Media Democracy

Media Democracy

How the Media Colonize Politics

THOMAS MEYER
with
Lew Hinchman

polity

First published in 2002 by Polity Press in association with Blackwell Publishing Ltd

Editorial office:
Polity Press
65 Bridge Street
Cambridge CB2 1UR, UK

Marketing and production:
Blackwell Publishing Ltd
108 Cowley Road
Oxford OX4 1JF, UK

Published in the USA by
Blackwell Publishing Inc.
350 Main Street
Malden, MA 02148, USA

A catalogue record for this book is available from the British Library.

Library of Congress Cataloging-in-Publication Data

Meyer, Thomas, 1943–
    Media democracy : how the media colonize politics / Thomas Meyer.
        p.   cm.
Includes bibliographical references and index.
        ISBN 0-7456-2843-5 – ISBN 0-7456-2844-3 (pbk.)
    1. Mass media – Political aspects.   I. Title.
        P95.8   .M493   2002
        302.23 – dc21

                                                                    2002002213

Typeset in 10.5 on 12 pt Sabon
by SNP Best-set Typesetter Ltd., Hong Kong
Printed in Great Britain by MPG Books, Bodmin, Cornwall

This book is printed on acid-free paper.

Contents

[handwritten notes: ∅, RE-READ CHAP. 1-2, & 4, (3?), 5, 6?? (1st October '13)]

Preface:
Media, Culture,
and Politics

Mass-media research

The mass media, their prospects and effects, their modes of operation and social consequences have all become key themes of social science, cultural criticism, and, ironically, of the media themselves within a remarkably short time. There are good reasons for social scientists and culture critics to pay attention: one can hardly think of another phenomenon that has shaped contemporary societies so thoroughly and durably, so profoundly and irreversibly. The increasing influence of contemporary mass media on modern life, in many areas a quite profound one, has been studied in considerable detail. Investigations have focused not only on communicative behavior itself, but also on its sociological consequences for central domains of life such as childhood, family, leisure-time behavior, and work.[1]

Social and media scientists have also intensively explored the transformations wrought by the mass media in the public and political spheres. Thus far three dimensions of the relation between the media and politics have especially preoccupied investigators:

First, they have studied the way the *public sphere* has been transformed as a result of changes in the mass-media communications, a process that embraces newspapers, television, the internet, and the "masses" themselves; in short, the ways in which public communication itself has been reshaped by the influence of the media.[2] They have demonstrated that in addition to the explicitly political media formats non-factual media have broadly expanded the terms of public debate.[3] The agenda-setting and agenda-building functions of modern mass media have played an especially prominent role here. However, in the course of media research it has also become evident that it would be a great mistake to identify the audiences of media products as such with the public. Publics emerge only in much more complex processes of information and discursive interaction of citizens.[4] Yet there can be no reasonable doubt of mass media's centrality in the process of shaping the public sphere.[5]

Second, concerning the relation between the media and political reality, research has been undertaken to understand the diverse patterns of the former in constructing the latter.[6] These analyses have shown more and more clearly how the mass media do not just mirror political life, but generate a political "reality" that is tailored to their own requirements.[7] The construction of reality by the mass media is a complex social process and all reports about political reality are inevitably affected by the criteria the media apply in selecting and presenting material, ones designed to secure maximum public response.

Third, research on the impact of the media has focused on the way their characteristic constructions of reality have affected the political orientations of their addressees.[8] Detailed studies on the effects of mass media present a wealth of confusing and contradictory data that seem to get fuzzier as the research methodology becomes more precise. In any case one has the impression that media studies are becoming so specialized that they can no longer be readily synthesized into a coherent picture. Nevertheless, this research has yielded some basic insights that may be useful in developing an empirically supported evaluation of the various assumptions, processes and consequences that condition the emergence in our time of a new political phenomenon: media democracy.[9]

Cultural studies

The research on the effects of mass media has born fruit in the form of theories concerning "videomalaise" and the "knowledge gap."[10] The former have studied suspected causal connections between frequent TV consumption and political alienation, but have not reached consensual conclusions. Whereas, e.g., T. Patterson has argued that news media have grown more negative and more cynical and thereby produced growing popular distrust of politicians and government, and even a general disengagement from civic life, P. Norris in a more recent comparative study insists that the general "videomalaise" argument has little empirical support.[11] The issue remains controversial. Surprisingly, the "knowledge gap" research has revealed that the spread of television consumption to more and more people involving larger segments of their time does not equalize the stock of politically relevant knowledge among subgroups of society, but instead widens such gaps between them.[12] Accordingly, the chances that equal rights to democratic participation can be secured through the spread and intensification of mass-media communication have grown slimmer.

Given the current state of the discipline, the one conclusion of media-impact research that appears most solidly grounded and most applicable across diverse fields of inquiry is this: the media do of course initiate the process of dissemination. However, in the last analysis, the individual members of the targeted audience bring with them certain knowledge, habits, interests and criteria of application that have a decisive bearing on the way in which media programming may affect them.[13] The media may thus offer their audience a variety of fare in many different ways, but the content will be only one input among many in shaping the citizens' powers of judgment. This argument, however, has been driven to its "postmodern" extreme by J. Fiske's concept of "semiotic democracy" which tends to dissolve the media text into its individual reading, so that the media themselves are not seen as being in a position to exert any real influence on their audiences' perception of the political sphere.[14]

In response to this S. Hall and D. Morley have sensitized us to the discovery that the active role of diverse recipients at the demand-side of mass-media communication by no means renders the supply-side structures of the media products irrelevant.[15] A vague concept of uses and gratifications in media reception that puts the blame for all kinds of deficiencies and shortcomings in the field of mediated political communication on the recipient's shoulders alone is not in tune with reality.[16] I agree with Corner's contention that, in the future, researchers should avoid concentrating exclusively on the micro-level processes involved in public reception of media programming. Doing so would mean drawing the wrong conclusions from previous studies.[17] Furthermore, a research approach stressing such micro-level reception would, by its very design, exempt the potential role of media power from scientific analysis. My study is a contribution to recovering empirically supported insights into the factors that influence the macro-level, i.e., the structural conditions that govern the pre-staging of events in the media theatre.

Depending on their social and individual background for large parts of the audiences the "preferred reading" (S. Hall) that is suggested by the immanent structure of the media products themselves is dominating their actual reading. And moreover, as will be shown in chapter 3 of this book, what matters most in the context of media democracy is the fact that the key actors of the political system always reckon with the effects of the preferred reading structures of media products on the large majority of the audience, and stage-manage their own performance in accordance with it.

Cultural studies and culture-critical analyses have also investigated basic changes in communicative behavior and orientation occasioned by modern mass media.[18] Authors such as N. Postman and B. Barber have pushed the critique of video culture toward a new and – for democratic theory – worrisome conclusion: that the citizens of television societies may be rapidly losing their faculties of political judgement as a result of the hegemony of stage-managed, entertainment-oriented presentations of events.[19] With much plausibility it has been argued that mass-media communication as a whole, by way of its modes of picking out or ignoring societal and political issues, has caused the aquiescence of the large majority of its audiences.[20] Political science has furthermore analyzed the extent to which the modern media may offer politicians and their staffs unprecedented opportunities to stage symbolic political events capable of winning citizens' adherence, and thereby may indirectly redistribute roles among the different actors in the political system.[21] Researchers have particularly directed attention to the symbiotic relationships that flow from the common interest political and media actors have in generating maximum publicity.[22]

Although Postman may be right that one basic reality of today's mass-media communications in the field of politics is the increasing tendency towards blurring the boundaries between journalism, entertainment, public relations, and advertising, it would, however, as Dahlgren argues, be both illusory and counter-productive to restrict the analysis to the condemnation of this new reality as such by striving for the rationalistic model of a public "uncontaminated by media culture".[23] Consequently, the interest underlying the concept of this book is rather to understand the empirical conditions under which these new mixed types of media discourses still contribute to appropriate political information and understanding, and those conditions under which they don't.

So far media research has concentrated mainly on these three out of the four dimensions of the relations between the mass media and politics: the relation between media discourses and audiences; the relation between media discourses and political realities; and the relation between mass media and the public sphere.

A new synthesis

What have been mostly neglected, however, are the far-reaching changes in political conditions that have resulted from the influence of the modern mass media and their peculiar logic of communication. Such analyses have in most cases been restricted to the communication side of the political system.[24] But the ways in which mass media influence the political system, the selection and shape of policies, and the entire political process reach much farther.[25] These effects of political mass communication on the deep structures of politics itself are the subject of this book. This book addresses the fourth dimension of the relation between media and politics, that of the repercussions media communication has on the substance of the political itself. Not only the communicative behavior of high-profile, "media star" politicians has been affected. In addition, there have been shifts in the whole nature of politics in media societies: the role and relative weight of the major actors such as parliaments and parties; the quality of the political process; and the selection of problem-solving strategies (policies) as well as the latter's prospects for success.[26] Staton has coined the term a "quantum leap of democracy" as a result of the complex interactions between politics and the mass media without analysing the emerging new phenomenon in concrete terms.[27] My crucial argument in support of the media democracy thesis of this book will be that the actors of the political system do not rely on a broad variety of different readings of the mainstream media texts by different audiences. Contrarily, in their own media-directed actions and discourses they conform most strictly to the codes of mainstream media, as if they were functioning as the only determinants for the audiences' reading and subsequent political behavior. Therefore, the step from party democracy to media democracy is the step from observation (of the most popular mass-media codes by the political system) to observance.

This book is intended to synthesize, in a critical, empirically oriented overview, the most significant results of media research, cultural studies and political science in order to contribute to the understanding of the transformation of the political sphere proper in modern media societies. Therefore its focus is not on audiences, media effects, or the complexities of the public sphere as a whole in modern media societies. The crucial question is, instead, how the essence of the political process is reshaped by the interplay of two processes: the way in which the media represent the political according to their own specific rules; and the way by which the nature of the political is transformed as a result of its ceaseless desire to submit to the power of these rules. At issue is the interplay between the media code and the political code. The goal will initially be to describe and explain the media-led processes that are transforming modern democracy. Subsequently, well-founded standards of democratic political theory will enable us to evaluate these processes as well.

An interdisciplinary approach

The present volume is based on an interdisciplinary research project at the University of Dortmund in Germany.[28] It brings together the most important findings of the disciplines mentioned above, supplemented by the results of my own studies carried out over a six-year period. I would like to thank the following colleagues for their productive and stimulating collaboration: communications scientists Professor Günter Rager and Professor Peter Ludes, sociologist Professor Hartmut Neuendorf, theater scholars Professor Erika Fischer-Lichte and Rüdiger Ontrup, MA, philosopher Dr Schicha, journalism graduates Carsten Brosda and Lars Rinsdorf, and political scientist Dr Udo Vorholt.

Our empirical research projects focused on two themes: first, the way in which political communications have become *theatrical* in modern media and in politics itself; second, the *interrelationships* between the *stage-managing* of the political in both of those spheres and the patterns of problem-solving behavior that have tended to emerge. Based on this research, the present study concludes that we are today witnessing a profound functional transformation of democracy in media societies. It touches not merely the level at which politics is portrayed or represented, but alters the political process itself in every one of its aspects. It is the central argument of this book that media democracy is a new political regime or constitution with its own rules, constraints, options, resources, channels of influence, and limitations. The individual chapters of this book will be devoted to their explication.

The structure of the book

The intention of the present study is to explain step by step why the laws of the media system (chapter 1) generally prevail when they collide with those of the political system (chapter 2). The latter submits to the media's "laws" for eminently political reasons (chapter 3). Political actors expect that they can recover some of the influence they have lost to the media over the way politics is presented in the public domain and thus over the conditions governing the attainment of legitimate authority. As a result some structures, functions and actors within the political system gain considerable influence: namely, those concerned with the way the political is "mediated" in both senses of the word (chapter 4). Meanwhile, others that were once near the center of events, such as parties and the entire intermediary sector of interest groups and associations, suffer a corresponding loss of influence in the larger political system (chapter 5). These circumstances give rise to a new form of politics: media democracy. It features a triangle consisting of the media public, political actors with high media profiles, and permanent opinion-polling, all of which reciprocally influence one another, and in which the consequences of the symbiotic interrelationships between media and politics become imbedded.[29]

From the viewpoint of modern democratic theory this transformation suggests three substantive questions, which will be explored once the necessary descriptive and analytical foundations have been laid. First, when politics is "mediated" – or presents itself in the media – does it lose its capacity to present information and guide rational reflection, or does it continue to inform and stimulate discussion, but now just in a new medium of expression (chapter 6)? Second, does the absorption of politics by the media enhance the quality of democratic participation by drastically expanding the public audience for political fare (chapter 5)? Third, should it be reckoned as a gain or loss for democracy, all things considered, that the broadening of the media public should have been achieved at the expense of a diminution in the role of parties and the intermediary system (chapter 6)?

Communicative culture and politics

No democracy worthy of the name can get by without a minimum of symmetry in the communicative links that connect the political leadership with the rank and file, or without a sufficiently developed public sphere for the flow of information and argument, or, finally, unless the communicative atmosphere of society promotes efforts to deliberate and reach consensus.[30] Thus, one of the supreme commandments of democratic theory and democratic politics is that citizens must carefully monitor developments in political communications, so that, in their role as citizens, they will be able to intervene in the political process should they desire to do so.

Much could be said in favor of the claim that, in societies shaped by the mass media, the mode of communication has become one of the dominant power structures, capable of exercising a decisive influence on all other societal institutions and processes.[31] The concrete form of the mode of communication that prevails in each case is defined both by the institutional context that governs the flow of communication, i.e., the communicative relationships, and by the communicative culture of the participants.

However, the communicative culture is not set in stone by the institutional context. Obviously, private/commercial media must at all costs follow the law that bids them maximize their audience. Different types of media will use all of their resources and capabilities in different ways to achieve this one end. In European countries with strong traditions of public broadcasting that have recently introduced private/commercial stations as well, there is a clear tendency for the former broadcasters to assimilate their programming, formats and *mise-en-scène* to those of their private competitors.[32] Thus, despite their considerable institutional differentiation, media systems tend to converge on a fundamentally similar communicative culture. Therefore, the present study, which investigates the relationships between media and political systems, focuses on the connection between the communicative culture and the political process rather than on institutional aspects of the media.

It should be emphasized from the outset that the media democracy thesis does not amount to a deterministic explanation. It concerns *opportunity structures* and the *mainstream cultures* that circumscribe the prevailing ways in which political actors may avail themselves of those opportunities. Though media codes increasingly influence how the political system may be reorganized to assert control over its media depictions, there are always other avenues open to political actors for responding to those codes. And of course, as Melucci has demonstrated, different audiences are free to make diverse uses of media products, just as social movements often have the power to challenge media codes that jeopardize their most cherished interests.[33]

The present study offers a different perspective from most others that have analyzed the nexus between mass media and politics. It focuses neither on how mass communications affect the public, nor on the complexity of the political public, nor even on the idiosyncracies, successes and failures of political media campaigns. Such questions, exhaustively treated in other studies, will furnish only points of reference for this one. Instead, the focus here will be on three crucial factors that have hitherto been somewhat neglected:

(a) the syntheses of information- and entertainment-oriented programming that may or may not conform to the requirements of democratic communication;
(b) the structural pre-staging built into staged media events;
(c) the effects of such a preliminary *mise-en-scène*, once integrated into the media theater, upon the substance of the political process in media democracy.

I will argue that the reciprocal interactions of these three factors have resulted in the emergence of a new regime, media democracy.

Defining the analytical concepts

Recent discussions of the role of the media in politics have focused on the central notions of *media democracy*,[34] *media society*,[35] and *mediacracy*.[36] The notion of *media democracy* has been most often invoked descriptively to shed light on a new political phenomenon; only secondarily has it been deployed normatively as a way of criticizing the media's tendency to undermine democracy's core claim to exercise legitimate authority. The term media democracy in this first sense refers to the ways in which the media have acquired a decisive role in the political process, above all in shaping public opinion and decision-making on political issues. We can then offer a descriptive account of the colonization of politics by the mass media whenever the internal rules peculiar to the media system encroach upon the political system, trumping or repealing the latter's own unique set of rules (chapter 3). The United States has proceeded farthest down this road, but other Western party democracies are rapidly catching up.

But one crucial unanswered question must be confronted right away: in what sense and to what degree (if at all) are democratic procedures jeopardized when the rules of the media system displace those of the political system? The answer of course depends entirely on the notion of democracy that underlies our judgments. To clarify this issue, the following analysis will invoke theories of democracy relevant to pluralistic party democracies (chapter 1). These theories will allow us to identify certain minimal criteria for the quality of public communicative relationships, which even media democracies would have to meet. In this way we arrive at well-founded standards for evaluating the quality of the public sphere as it has been shaped by the media, a task we take up toward the end of the study (chapter 6; conclusion).

In the analysis that follows an attempt will be made to clarify what actually happens in the communications processes of the mass media, what determines their outcomes, and how they influence the political sphere. The point is to enable us to better understand and evaluate the democratic qualities of media democracy. In our view it is a *novel regime* in which political actions are systematically legitimized by being subjected to the rules of the media system.

The notion of *mediacracy* goes a step beyond that of media democracy, since it includes a specific diagnosis of political and cultural circumstances.[37] The mediacracy thesis claims that the media's programming decisions cater almost exclusively to the political and cultural tastes of the broad mainstream of society, which, because they are exactly mirrored in media fare, seem always to be confirmed and reinforced in a self-validating hypothesis. The characteristics of mediacracy are present, then, whenever the mass media act as a mediator and catalyst, turning the public's preferences and inclinations, its limited attention-span and need for information into a kind of fundamental law governing all dimensions of public communication. We shall therefore have occasion in this volume to examine the media's peculiar double standard: inclusion of the greatest number of users; yet exclusion of productions that cater to tastes outside the mainstream. Accordingly, a central concern of this study is to ascertain what these findings imply for political communication and for the way democracy actually works in a modern media society.

Our current state of knowledge certainly entitles us to conclude that the rules of the media system now dominate the political sphere.[38] But it is another matter altogether to determine whether – and to what extent – we might in the future succeed in creating a new synthesis between the rules of the media system and the requirements of the political sphere that would allow us to achieve appropriate levels of information and political argument. Yet another unresolved issue touches on the mediocrity that marks the typical contents of today's media productions. Is it irrevocably tied to the dominance of the media's communicative rules, or is it characteristic only of the way they are currently applied and therefore open to change?

We conclude the text by examining just this issue, since the way it is resolved will indicate how much leeway there is to improve the communicative practices of modern democracy (chapter 6).

1

The Logic
of Politics

Democratic communication

Objectives and functions

Democracy is not possible without a functioning political public sphere that puts the individual in a position to decide and act autonomously. That much, very few people would wish to dispute. But we have no self-evident criteria that would allow us to stipulate what minimum autonomy requirements would have to be maintained in order for democracy to exist at all. This reservation is true in both a quantitative and qualitative sense. Political-science research has come up with various notions of democracy that are worlds apart in respect to the criteria they employ to evaluate levels of political participation and the quality of political communication. Can we glimpse behind these different perspectives some minimum set of standards that all would agree must be fulfilled if there is going to be a democracy?[1]

Dahlgren has argued that the political public sphere displays four dimensions: (a) media institutions; (b) media representation; (c) social structure; (d) sociocultural interaction.[2] In present-day media societies television plays the dominant, paradigmatic role in the institutional domain, one that pervades and stamps all of the other media. Of course, this generalization should not lead us to overlook the continuing, though episodic, relevance still maintained by those other media, even the "mini-media" of the intermediary sector and civil society. The social structure comes into play chiefly by differentiating the behavior of the audience in assimilating media programming.

Different audiences make sense of media messages in diverse ways, partly as a result of the social strata to which they belong. Sociocultural interaction is a term that pertains to the sphere of face-to-face communication typical of the life-world and civil society. The way citizens in the life-world respond to media messages and other communicative inputs will decide whether they end up as informed participants capable of making acute political judgments.

Relying on Ray's empirical studies, we must assume that a broad stratum of politically ill-informed and uninterested citizens will count as non-discussants.[3] These are citizens who are not inclined to engage in social conversation (face-to-face interaction) about the political messages to which they have been exposed. Because of the passive way in which they assimilate media fare, they are the ones, as Hall would put it, who will most likely respond positively to the "preferred reading" of the messages encoded in media texts. In light of previous research on the reception of media texts it would seem justified to assume that those texts themselves provide a powerful input to *everyone* exposed to them, one that influences all further communication. And for the not insignificant contingent of non-discussants, whose numbers vary from society to society and case to case, media texts play a decisive role in shaping their understanding of the political world. That is one of the most important reasons why the present study focuses on the contributions mass-media input (media representation) can make to an appropriate grasp of the political in media democracies. In pursuing this perplexing question, we must first try to clarify what appropriateness means: our criterion consists in asking whether the aspect of the political thematized in any given instance has been adequately represented in media texts, such that a reasonable member of the media audience could identify the political content *as* political, in terms of its own inherent logic (chapter 1, pages 10–16).

The other reason for concentrating on the political implications of media content has already been mentioned in connection with the media democracy thesis that is so fundamental to this volume. Empirical analysis shows that actors in the political system are increasingly dependent on media codes, not just in designing their political communications but across the whole gamut of their conduct. They tend to assume that they can only count on exerting control over their portrayal in the mass media, thus gaining access (on their terms) to a broad public, if they submit to the established media codes. But there is an implicit tension between media codes and the logic of the political. Much depends on correctly understanding the nature of that tension, since it poses a perennial obstacle to achieving a successful synthesis between the media codes and the logic of the political. The latter, which we shall reconstruct in the following pages, can serve as a reliable touchstone for judging whether or not the media representation of the political is appropriate.

In laying out the relationship between democratic communication and political logic in this and the next two sections (pages 7–16), we will emphasize three fundamental questions about democracy and its context. First, what are the minimum levels of information and communication that the political public has to attain in order to make possible a kind of civic communication appropriate to modern democracy and to the citizens' own well-founded self-understanding? Second, how can mass media, especially their flagship, television, contribute to a democratically appropriate level of information and communication, and how can we define this contribution? And finally, how can a functioning party democracy contribute to a culture that puts a premium on communication and participation? What will the decline of parties mean for the communicative political culture of a democratic society? The answers to these questions would deliver a reliable yardstick to measure the quality of media communication in the political sphere.

Classical theories of democracy generally define it as a system of institutions, a set of procedures for discussion and decision-making, and, in some cases, as a path to certain outcomes.[4] All of these definitional elements involve a certain mode of communication that is suited to democracy and in turn depends on the prevailing communicative relationships. Pluralist democracies based on the rule of law share a range of crucial characteristics, no matter what their specific constitutions may be. Besides the indispensable guarantees of basic human rights and popular sovereignty as the ultima ratio, pluralist democracies usually display a number of other institutions: a multi-party system, parliamentary procedures, an independent judiciary, freedom of the press (and other media) and a willingness to tolerate highly varying forms and levels of active civic participation. Given widespread agreement on such fundamental issues, differences on other matters such as the advantages of different party or electoral systems, parliamentary versus presidential systems, and adversarial versus consociational democracy play only a subordinate role. Practical experience also shows that aspirations toward constitutional government, pluralism and the rule of law are only realized when civil societies emerge with a lively, diversified institutional life. A network of what Tocqueville called intermediary bodies, i.e., associations, interest groups, organizations and citizens' initiatives, must arise to mediate continually between society and the political system.[5] The structure and function of the political public sphere as well as of the mass media that shape it have to be evaluated in the light of the strong requirements of this sort of pluralistic, constitutional democracy, and not simply by reference to some isolated criterion such as whether or not free elections are guaranteed.

The case of Germany may be of special interest here, because the Federal Constitutional Court has validated this strong principle of democratic accountability through a number of closely reasoned opinions involving both public and private media, although one must of course recognize the limits of what law can achieve in cases like these. In its decisions the Court has articulated a principle that, while oddly vague, turns out to be appropriately targeted and far-reaching in its effects. It has been incorporated into the charters of the German public broadcasting networks as well as the media laws of the German federal states. Ideally, the mass media would contribute to democratic communication in a number of ways: balanced and comprehensive reporting, objectivity and respect for persons, fidelity to the truth in form, content, and style of coverage, as well as a manner of presenting events that encourages all citizens to participate in public communication. These norms are far-reaching, in that they depict a nearly ideal communicative situation; yet they are also quite vague, since it is not clear how or to what degree they should be applied in the real world of mass communications. Nevertheless, they are appropriately targeted, since they describe the requisite mode of communication with sufficient precision. Whether we can render them concrete in the context of communications policy depends largely on the ideal of democracy that we choose to pursue in our social practices, politics and in the mass media themselves.

Basic models of democracy

The norms of democratic politics, as they are applied to pluralistic, law-governed polities, demarcate a broad spectrum of possibilities within which there is ample room for different models of democratic participation. This holds true even in cases where competing political actors try to yoke the constitutional framework of their respective commonwealths to their own political projects. There are three theoretical paradigms that enable us to define alternative approaches to participation in real-world politics: the model of *democracy as a marketplace*, the model of *participatory democracy*, and the model of a *democratic civil society*. All of them can legitimately claim to have specified what democracy in modern societies means in actual practice.

The market model of democracy has been dubbed by its advocates the "realistic theory of democracy," as if any idea of democratic participation that went beyond what this model provides were inherently utopian, incapable of coming to terms with the complex realities of modern-day societies. Originally developed in the work of Josef Schumpeter and Anthony Downs, the market model postulates that a political system satisfies the conditions of democratic legitimacy so long as it meets one minimal requirement: the individual voter must have the opportunity to choose between at least two sets of competing political elites.[6] The model says nothing about the connection between elite policies and the real interests, motives and intentions of the ordinary citizen, nor does it specify the extent to which citizens should be given a chance to participate in the decisions that elites make once they are in office. As its name suggests, the market model takes its cue from classical economic theory, which assumes a market in goods and services where self-interested individual decisions are automatically harmonized to achieve the general welfare. Applied to politics, the model holds that the mere presence of a choice among elites is sufficient to meet the democratic desideratum that political action should yield policies likely to maximize the common good of society.

Although political elites, in competing for the favor of the electorate, may be pursuing only their own private interests in power, prestige, and income, they presumably cannot succeed in doing so unless they present to the public, and then subsequently carry out, a program of political action that a potential majority would be willing to support as an expression of its own political interests. If the invisible hand of the elite and voter market is to effect such a convergence of conflicting interests, one central condition has to be met: access to information. To be sure, the extent to which potential voters will in fact try to obtain information about electoral alternatives and the records of the elite candidates depends on how great the benefits are that they expect to reap from the victory of the party they prefer. And this is exactly the reason why the available information about the candidates' electoral platforms, previous accomplishments, and records has to be comprehensive, reliable, easily accessible and complete. Otherwise the price individual voters would have to pay in time and effort to make informed judgments would be far too high. If such information were not generally available, even this minimal model of democracy could not live up to its own self-proclaimed standards of legitimacy. So, although it has reduced requisite participation levels to an absolute minimum, and assigned no significant role to public deliberation and consensus, the market model must meet very high standards for providing reliable information about the reality of politics to the public.

The model of participatory democracy is a type of representative and highly institutionalized democracy which puts a premium on sustained and significant participation in decision-making on the part of a large number of active citizens at all levels of the political system's institutions, but especially at the intermediate level of political parties, associations and grass-roots initiatives emanating from civil society.[7] According to this model, a prerequisite of claims to legitimacy in a democratic society is that the citizens themselves not only participate in elections, but also formulate and defend their own interests in whichever organizations, political parties or committees they see as most appropriate and promising. When it comes to decisions affecting society as a whole, civic leagues such as interest groups, associations, grass-roots citizens' lobbies, churches and parties must occupy the middle ground between the political and social systems. It is these associations that have to provide opportunities for the vast majority of citizens to participate in a sustained way in democratic decision-making even at the highest levels. There must also be opportunities for people to have a say in the decisions that affect their everyday lives and work environments, for example in the voluntary associations of civil society and grass-roots initiatives, in social and political self-help projects at the local level, or through workplace democracy along the lines practiced in some countries such as Germany, Sweden or France.

To make democratic participation a reality, social and political organizations have to accommodate their members' demands to have a say; but at the same time, the citizens themselves must be willing to participate. This model of democracy may therefore be further distinguished from the market model in that it foresees permanent active participation in all kinds of political organizations, and, in addition, the creation of forums for direct communication among the participants in and around the relevant organizations. Rather than merely providing centers for obtaining and processing information, organizations would – according to this participatory model – try to deliberate with the hope of achieving consensus about the goals and approaches of action in common.

The third model, grass-roots democracy or "civil society" as a compehensive concept for the polity can be distinguished from that of participatory democracy in at least one key respect: the former does not expect much in the way of democracy from institutions or big organizations, such as parties and the political system. Instead, democratic participation and decision-making are supposed to be confined, in the final analysis, to the domains of civil society and the life-world, where the smaller scale insures that unrestricted citizen involvement and supervision of decision-making are still possible.[8] The only way to generate a democratic commonwealth on a larger scale, whether for society as a whole or even the entire globe, would be through horizontal networking among the many grass-roots citizens' lobbies. Even though the notion of a global network of such grass-roots citizens' lobbies ("civil society") is familiar to the advocates of this model, they still see in civil society the true arena for democratic deliberation and decision just because it is local. Those who attend neighborhood assemblies can have a dialogue about goals and approaches, and find ways to implement and oversee the decisions they have reached. Even more than in the model of participatory democracy, the actual practices of processing information, forming judgments, and deliberating to reach a consensus shift to the level of small circles of engaged citizens. Of course, these citizens are just as dependent on accurate information about politics and society on a macro-level, as are those whose actions are addressed to the more formal institutions of the political system. Focus on the opportunities for face-to-face communication does not rule out – indeed it even presupposes – the possibility that the participating citizens can acquire wide-ranging information about the political system from the mass media.

Minimal requirements for political communication

All of these models are compatible with the normative claims of Western democracy even though controversies might arise concerning their feasibility. They all concur in stipulating that comprehensive, reliable information about – and drawn from – the political and

social systems has to be made available. What distinguishes them
is the extent to which they insist on having something more: an
additional public space for dialogue, deliberation, and consensus-
building. All of them assume that citizens will have complete, undistorted information about the most important political issues as well
as about the intentions and programs of the political actors who represent them. The participatory and civil society models, respectively
though in different ways, further assume that there should be an
extensive system of opportunities for participants to communicate
and try to achieve consensus, and that they should have a role in
shaping decisions about the political affairs that concern them.

Party democracy is the most prominent and widespread form of
participatory democracy, at least in terms of how the latter is
described by political science and is generally supposed to work in
Western Europe.[9] In respect to political communication and the
public sphere, party democracy unquestionably requires a political
culture of information, one that conveys to the citizen an appropriate understanding of the programmatic alternatives elaborated by
competing parties. In this regard the notion of party democracy
differs little from the pure elite competition models proposed by
"realistic" democratic theory. Yet, as Sarcinelli has shown, it also
offers something else: the opportunity for internal, semi-public and
public forums in which face-to-face communication and political
deliberation are possible.[10] For party members and non-members
alike, such forums have a public significance that goes far beyond
any mere PR function they may otherwise possess. Above all, party
democracy offers an opportunity of still greater value to its own
members and even (albeit in a less robust form) to the members of
organizations within the intermediary sector and civil society that
lobby the parties: the chance to combine political communication
with political decision-making in an institutional setting. To be sure,
this latter point is most persuasive in the case of parties that participate in government, although even opposition parties offer similar
opportunities in a weaker form. They too must offer programs that
reflect the views of members and fellow-travelers. In a democratic
system the opposition programs may some day become official policy,
so members can indeed hope to influence political decision-making
even before their chosen party actually participates in a governing
coalition. For all these reasons functioning party democracies have
an essential influence on the quality of political communication. Not
only do they presuppose high-quality communication, but they can

also help initiate it. This would be much less true of the American party system, since parties there are weaker and far more dependent on the campaign contributions of wealthy donors and interest groups, and in any case rarely offer coherent programs.

Social scientist Friedhelm Neidhardt has described three functions that public communication has to fulfill at an appropriate level if there is going to be a genuinely democratic public sphere, regardless of how broadly or narrowly one understands the meaning of democracy.[11] First, it must exhibit transparency; that is, every citizen needs a chance to see and understand what is going on in politics and the crucial social processes that are related to it. Information has to be comprehensive, accurate and reliable. Second, Neidhardt adds a validation function. Citizens who are so inclined should be able to evaluate the validity of their own positions in light of the relevant but different opinions, themes and stocks of information that others hold. Finally, public communication has an orienting function. The public realm should encourage an interplay among different sources of information and argument. Their juxtaposition will give rise to public opinion, which can then provide individual citizens with a clear point of orientation for their own views.

A structure of public, political communication that does not adequately fulfill these basic functions may still contribute something to the integration of the social system by bringing certain common themes into wide currency, thus reinforcing the social ties among disparate individuals. It may even contribute something to the perpetuation of a society with democratic institutions and to this extent apparently serve the interests of democracy. Nevertheless, it deprives these institutions of the very political communicative culture they need to make good on their democratic aspirations in actual practice. Thus, public communication in a democracy has to be tailored to the distinctive logic of the political process that takes place in the larger context of society, despite its characteristic method of seizing the public's attention by selective presentation and abbreviation of content. For citizens can only acquire relevant information from the media about policies that concern them if the media depict the political process in all its diverse dimensions and facets. Though the mass media never occupy the whole of the public sphere they contribute tremendously to its shape and play the central part in its making. Thus, their role in and for democracy must consist in making appropriate political information and evaluation possible for all citizens. If public communication in a society cannot, in principle, fulfill this condition, then no one can make a serious claim that it is democratic. In any event guarantees of free elections and the elite competition that they enable do not suffice to make good the promise of democracy.

Political logic

The importance of the logic of the political process for political communications within a democracy is not simply due to any dogmatic claims for correct representation that may be raised by political scientists, but for another obvious reason. To the extent that its characteristics are fairly closely approximated in any given situation, the logic of the political process inevitably implies a certain standard of how the media should report about politics. These are what we may call the conditions of appropriateness for political reportage. For whatever construction the media code may try to impose on the political events to be represented, however much it may attempt to transform them, in the end the logic of the events themselves has to shine through in the media's finished product. A radically constructivist position that disputes this simple requirement is not only inadequate as a theory; it also runs aground on empirical reality. Empirical investigations made by the Dortmund research project have shown unambiguously that the constructivist claims are incorrect.[12] The most diverse kinds of political stage-management carried out by the media can indeed be more or less appropriate to their subject matter in the sense just described. What then is the essence of this political logic that appropriate media coverage is supposed to capture?

Political processes have a distinctive character that sets them apart from the logic inscribed in the course of processes occurring elsewhere, in other systems of social action.[13] To communicate about politics in an appropriate way means, in the first instance, to understand this logic and never to lose sight of it amid all its transformations by the mass media. This holds true no matter what level we are talking about: international relations, domestic policy, or even politics outside of formal institutions, e.g. interest groups. In order to meet the standards of democratic politics, the mass media have to communicate political events in their own fashion, to bring out the characteristic features of every event they report. And political processes do indeed have a logic all their own, even though the particular factors that reciprocally affect one another – interests, values, power resources, legitimacy, relevant institutions – can always be weighted differently, or come into play in various ways. Ascertaining and gaging what role the different factors of political logic may play, or what elements of it the public already knows or dismisses as irrelevant, is something that can only be done under the pressure of concrete events. Developing a sense of how to handle these problems, and thus helping citizens understand what may be of special relevance to their range of choices in any given case, is at all events the decisive challenge for mass media that aspire to play a role in creating a democratic public sphere.

Factors and dimensions of politics

The logic of the political is indeed an indispensable analytical tool for understanding politics, in whatever context it may occur. This is true on a theoretical level because it provides basic concepts and models that enable us to understand, elaborate, and evaluate our observations about politics in ways suited to its intrinsic nature. But it also provides practical guidelines for journalists to interpret events and then communicate their essential features to enlighten citizens about what really transpires in the realm of politics.

Politics in the broadest sense always goes on in three dimensions: *polity*, *policy*, and *political* process. Polity designates the foundations of the commonwealth as definitively established for a given period of time, including its written and unwritten norms and rules. Constitutions and systems of rules regulating the political process form part of the polity as do the political cultures of the different milieus that together make up a political community. Although these constitutive elements always give the political process meaning and direction, even where they are not sufficiently precise to guide decision-making, they frequently lie concealed beneath the surface of day-to-day politics and thus escape the notice of most observers. The recount dilemma that followed the US presidential elections of November 7, 2000 illuminated, as if by a sudden lightning strike, how vital both elements are – the written rules and the ingrained political culture – in enabling us to understand a political event. The antiquated mechanism of an indirect vote via the electoral college, in which most state delegations give all their electoral votes to the candidate who won a plurality in that state, is what first triggered this confusing débâcle. Until the recount crisis very few observers, domestic or foreign, really knew much about these arcane rules. But in any case it was the political culture of the United States, or more precisely two cherished principles within it, that permit us to make sense of the whole affair: every vote should count; and the loser should graciously concede defeat. Because these two principles collided during the recount, the political actors, their impetuous staffs and the various courts involved were all forced into sometimes grotesque and self-contradictory positions as they tried to do justice to both at once. Reports that failed to bring all this background knowledge into the clear light of day did more to disseminate misinformation than to clarify events. It is a matter of journalistic discretion to decide just how much of the taken-for-granted framework of action needs to be presumed, omitted or made explicit. In the individual case that decision can be sensibly reached only when one knows precisely which factors are involved and in what ways. Although they too are subject to change, and thus often the targets of political decision-making, these factors still limit what political actors can attempt to do.

Except in borderline cases of vacuous, merely symbolic action done for show, politics in the broad sense always involves a policy dimension. This is the effort to find solutions for politically defined problems by means of programs for action, which identify and apply the means that seem best suited to handle them. As a rule, interests and values shape our ideas about the appropriate solutions to problems, and give us a way to choose a preferred alternative from among the many possibilities.

The third dimension encountered wherever politics goes on is that of the political process, i.e., the effort to gain official acceptance of one's chosen program of action. Within a given context of action, diverse actors will advance various interests, try to make them appear legitimate by citing convincing reasons for adopting them, and pursue strategies of compromise, consensus-building, or rallying a majority behind their programs. For the actors, the point is to use a range of political resources to enhance the likelihood (given the limits of what they can reasonably hope to achieve) that their proposed solutions will be officially adopted. Among the resources that count politically are socio-economic power, publicity, prestige, money, threats of sanctions, claims to legitimacy that might garner public support, and, now more than ever, the media charisma or appeal of the main political actors, especially salient in an age of media democracy.

Politics always takes place within these three dimensions, and in the interplay of the factors at work in each one. It is undoubtedly true that the concepts we use to characterize these factors are analytic: constructed by scientific observers for the purpose of explaining the course of political events. Still, we can think of them as quasi-empirical concepts, since they can be checked against experience, modified and refuted. They epitomize and cross-relate factors at work in the real world, ones that emerge and influence the political process itself. We can call the ensemble of these three dimensions, along with the factors they describe and their patterns of interaction, the logic of politics, as distinguished, say, from the logic of economic or cultural processes. That logic is always at the center of the structure and dynamics of political events, but it has to be employed with due regard to the variety of empirical circumstances. One can never just mechanically apply a model that has been preconceived and specified down to the last detail. An appropriate journalistic account of political reality, selective and stage-managed as it invariably always will be, needs, nonetheless, to represent in some way or another the relevant features of the political logic of the events it relates to. This is a basic requirement for its appropriateness.

Instructive borderline cases

Some of the most interesting aspects of political logic, both for enabling us to understand it more precisely and for getting a firmer grasp of actual political events, are those that involve borderline cases in which one dimension of the political seems to be missing. There are two clearly defined situations in which the policy dimension appears to have lost its constitutive role and therefore ceased to have any relevance in shaping the course of political events: the cases of revolution and civil war. In both instances a significant portion of the citizenry abandons the commonwealth's established system of political order. Citizens who cling to the old system may receive violent treatment from those who intend to establish a new order outside the erstwhile rules of the game. Thus within the always limited, frequently quite short span of time that a revolution lasts, there are in a sense two rival commonwealths contending with each other in the territory previously occupied by a single unified, formerly legitimate association. The point of their conflict is for one or the other to introduce a new order of things: new procedures, norms, and goals that will be binding on all concerned. Within each of these rival groups, of course, binding norms and rules do prevail, even in the period of transition. But the questions of whether the feuding groups can continue to live together in a shared political commonwealth, and which of the competing sets of rules will eventually prevail, may remain unresolved for quite some time. In this sense, then, even in a situation where the form and content of the polity is a bone of contention, and the generally binding framework of order is temporarily put out of commission, the polity dimension remains in effect for each of the groups involved. At the same time, the polity dimension becomes one of policy, i.e., it becomes a controversial issue that has to be resolved. Polity thus seems to play a peculiar double role in the constitution of the political process, though only for brief periods.

The standard case of issueless politics

There are some political systems in which, strictly speaking, no political process at all seems to be taking place. These include all systems that have developed strategies to avoid politics. When they are operating in accordance with their own intrinsic standards, such systems feature a single center of power and decision-making that is insulated from public discussion, discourages the inclusion of multiple actors from outside the leadership cadre, and is immune to the mandates of critical public opinion. In place of a political process, decisions are made by fiat, both to identify what problems require solution, and to specify which potential solutions are acceptable. There are in this respect structural parallels among the several different strategies of politics avoidance: ethical traditionalism, technocracy and fundamentalism. In the twentieth century, totalitarian systems such as German National Socialism and Stalinist Communism practiced structurally similar forms of the fundamentalist strategy. In the heyday of Stalinism the dictator alone decided which policy proposals would make it onto the agenda, which implementation strategies would be selected, which interests were to be consulted, and which opinions and values were to be considered or ignored. From all outward appearances it was impossible to discern any sort of regular political process going on. There were no signs that alternative courses of action were ever weighed, different actors allowed to submit their plans, or various strategies of action and social power-resources permitted to mobilize. At most, only vestigial forms of the political process remained, and these only at the very center of political power. However, a reconstruction of events based on research in the primary sources always reveals that a regular political process was indeed going on all the time, albeit largely hidden from the eyes of outside observers. In the media democracies of our own age cases of so-called "issueless politics" are becoming increasingly common.[14] The notion of issueless politics refers to stage-managed events that lack in real terms what has been publicly proclaimed as their policy dimension. For example, when a government official calls a press conference in the capital with great media fanfare and declares that this or that issue is going to be "a top priority," he has in fact just staged a political event devoid of the usual characteristics of the policy dimension: a plan of action with a specific content and problem-solving approach that can be critically examined.

The same pattern may be observed in the case of a ribbon-cutting ceremony for the opening of a new factory in a region of high unemployment, to which media representatives have been invited. The rituals and images are designed to create the impression of a causal link between political action and reduced levels of unemployment, even though the political actor who is the beneficiary of the stage-managed "media event" may actually have done nothing at all to bring the factory to the area, or even have lived up to his self-proclaimed goal of pursuing effective job-creation measures. In a notorious American example of issueless politics, the 1988 Republican presidential candidate, George Bush Sr, successfully associated his Democratic opponent, Michael Dukakis, with a convicted killer named Willie Horton, who had been given a weekend furlough in Dukakis' home state of Massachusetts and was then rearrested on a second murder charge. Even though Bush had no specific plan for crime reduction, and even though Dukakis had not created Massachusetts' parole program or had anything to do with Horton's release, Bush's campaign staff still managed to create the impression that Dukakis was somehow "soft on criminals," which undoubtedly contributed to Bush's subsequent victory.

This sort of symbolic "placebo politics," deliberately crafted to take advantage of the laws of media influence, creates the illusion that concrete programs of action have been or will be carried out, when in terms of "real" instrumental action nothing whatever has been done.[15] In such cases the policy level is converted into an element in the political process, in which the goals are acquiring legitimacy, safeguarding one's own power, and lulling the public into complacency about existing problems. There is no serious effort to make policy. Political matters are limited to the levels of polity and the political process, while the dimension of policy, paraded for its value as show, has been subordinated to the broader objectives of gaining legitimacy and playing down real problems. It may not always be possible to determine in specific instances whether the policy dimension has become entirely irrelevant or only partly so, but it plays no constitutive role at all in cases of political action such as the ones described above. Nevertheless, it is characteristic of issueless politics that the policy dimension should be acted out or simulated, so that, in the minds of most observers, it will seemingly continue to play the same constitutive role that it normally would. This borderline case demonstrates that, at least in the ordinary understanding of legitimate politics, the policy dimension cannot be omitted. It remains an indispensable component of political claims to legitimacy under all circumstances. It is a mark of the emergence of modern media democracy that this borderline case has acquired increasing salience, and has by now become a recurrent feature of politics, the illusory quality of which the average observer usually has trouble seeing.

The domain of political reality has dynamic factors at work in it that roughly correspond to the three dimensions of the political. These factors can be defined and partly described by means of those dimensions, and thus reconstructed in theory. When we get into detailed cases, we may find that they have been given varying linguistic and taxonomic expression; different authors will not always describe them in the same ways or the same words. Still, when we shift from words to their referents, we find a widely shared consensus in political science about the factors that are always involved in the real course of politics. The ways in which they unavoidably interact with one another shape the characteristic logic of the political. As long as media constructions claim to convey political realities, rather than merely serving as the occasion or excuse for empty media events staged by the media or by politicians themselves, they must shed light on the strands of political logic at work in them. That is one prerequisite for their factual accuracy that can never be circumvented, no matter how cleverly media experts may tweak their political themes.

Party democracy

Pluralist democracy is multi-party democracy, regardless of whether its normative claims and public self-interpretation tend to follow the minimalist market model, i.e., the economics-derived theory of democracy, or a participatory understanding of it. The European democracies, in contrast to the US political system, all see themselves as participatory party democracies. European parties are not simply organizations that mobilize for elections and then go dormant, like American parties. Through their membership organizations and the mediating role they play between civil society and the political system, they are supposed to ensure a continuing effective participation of a large number of active citizens in the process of political opinion-formation in the periods between elections.[16] Thus, vital and democratic political parties are at the center of participatory democracy as it is claimed by European political theory and publics.

Norms and claims of multi-party democracy

In none of its developmental phases has party democracy in Europe ever quite lived up to its reputation, whether the barbed descriptions by its critics or abstract models elaborated by scholars. The German case is revealing because of extensive legislation in the matter. Through much of German history until World War II, critics clung to the authoritarian maxim that parties would only wreck the state if they should ever acquire any real influence in – or over – it. The state was understood in the tradition of Hegel as having its own unique responsibilities which it could carry out properly only if it occupied a position above society. That is why, even as late as the Weimar Republic's constitution, parties are mentioned only as entities that had to be kept at arm's length and isolated, symbolically at least, from the sphere of legitimate state business. The reality of party activity in the Weimar Republic never matched these constitutional pretensions. But at the very end of the Republic, in the final stage of democracy's collapse, the president of the Reich did try to save the state, or so he thought, by wresting power from the traditional parties and handing it over to a party – actually a movement – that would never tolerate any rivals. That organization, which aspired to be both a party in the old sense and yet to rise above all parties, was determined to put an end to democracy, along with the other parties that had sustained it, as thoroughly and rapidly as possible once it had the power to do so. The history of the newly established democracy of the German Federal Republic was initiated in a conscious break with the traditions of the authoritarian state and the old anti-party sentiments, and as an opening toward the democratic standards of other Western democracies.

Germany's new Constitution, the Basic Law, did recognize political parties, but the applicable provisions seemed to assign them only a modest role. The historic tension between the classical liberal and the modern pluralistic democratic roles of political parties is still evident in some of its provisions. Article 21 expressed the expectation that the parties would help shape the formation of public opinion on political matters. They were the only organizations in society to be granted such a constitutional privilege. Yet that privilege appeared to conflict with Article 38, which provided that deputies in the parliament should not function as the representatives of parties, but should instead represent the entire nation and be accountable solely to their own consciences. These clauses of Article 38 seemed to exempt the deputies from any legally binding control by the parties, a conclusion which has led to heated debates in political science and constitutional jurisprudence about the tension between the two Articles.

These controversies featured three distinct positions. Some scholars supposed that there was no conceivable alternative to the parties' dominance in molding public opinion, so they interpreted the restrictions in Article 38 as an attempt to strengthen the hand of party representatives in parliament against potential efforts to impose internal discipline on them. Others insisted that the individual deputy's role should be seen in light of the liberal tradition, in which the parliament was an assembly of local dignitaries, and the parties were limited to supplying help and organizational support in the process of shaping public opinion on political matters. A third position saw the tension-laden relationship between the party function and the personal discretion of the deputies as one that the Constitution had deliberately tried to foster. The Basic Law was then supposedly creating a framework within which the two aspects of a deputy's role would provide mutual stimulation, while also checking and balancing one another.

Gerhard Leibholz, a justice on Germany's Constitutional Court but also a political scientist who has done much to shape emerging paradigms of constitutional jurisprudence on this issue, proposed a persuasive "realist" interpretation. In his view the law should take into account the reality of the influence of parties on politics such as we have observed it up through the 1990s. According to his analysis political parties in the complex territorial states of our time supplied the modern equivalent of plebiscitary democracy. By voting for a given party, the people were allegedly deciding on a choice of a direction among competing policy-alternatives, and thus entrusting their advocates with the task of translating their choice into practice, with

as few revisions as possible, in the form of legislation and government action. On this interpretation the democratic role of parties was
primarily a matter of presenting concrete alternatives clearly spelled
out in their programs, and only secondarily of recruiting and overseeing the personnel who would be responsible for implementing
them.

Underlying Leibholz' notion of democracy, i.e., that parties offer
policy direction in a *de facto* plebiscite, is the surmise that the profound pluralism of values and interests that characterizes modern
society is in principle insuperable.[17] Given a permanent division
over values, the only way to safeguard a degree of popular control
inherent in the tradition of direct democracy is to make sure pluralism is reflected in what competing parties offer to voters, and that
the formation of opinion at the level of the state faithfully articulates
the pluralistic interests of the electorate. Under these circumstances
society as a whole can be represented only when the various parties
govern in turn, with the opposition supplanting the previous governing party and its programs after a reasonably short interval. This
model attaches such great significance to the interplay of majority
and minority, the alternation of parties in power, and thus the
clash of clear programmatic alternatives, precisely because it inter-
prets democracy in light of the parties' plebiscitary function. As
understood by Leibholz, elections in a party democracy are not
supposed to be choices among persons, but among the concrete
policies they endorse.

Constraints and deficits of
party democracy

Party democracy as practiced in most European societies until
recently did correspond, though only in rough approximation, to the
image of it discussed above. Yet even in its prime party democracy
suffered from two major defects. First, the party leadership always
had the upper hand over the rank-and-file as well as the party apparatus. At no time did the parties ever simply function as discursive
communities capable of transmitting their articulated will to the political system. Second, it was never the case that a program unambiguously adopted in a plebiscite could just be rammed through the
parliament and government. The alternative programs presented to
the public were always rather unspecific, although those in most
European party democracies did consistently exhibit clear-cut differ-

ences on certain points. All this meant that many if not most of the policies that the parties actually enacted as binding decisions once they got into power had never previously been tested in the clear light of public attention and controversy. Furthermore, in a political system with proportional representation such as Italy, Sweden or Germany, majorities can usually only be formed through coalition-building. Far-reaching compromises thus had to be made to accommodate the interests and ideas of the coalition's junior partner, which entailed that few voters (of the coalition's largest party) could ever discern in the actions of the new parliament and government the sort of policies for which they thought they had given a whole-hearted mandate. Despite these reservations it remains true that the choice among parties is usually a selection among alternative policy directions.

Among the advanced Western democracies one might hesitate in applying this thesis to the United States party system. There parties are essentially local and state organizations with only weak and intermittent ties to national party committees. The latter have no way to impose a common program or set of policy principles on the local and state organizations or – even more important – on the candidates who run under the party's banner. Each candidate is a political entrepreneur who relies on his or her own staff and fund-raising skills to rise to prominence and win primary elections. Once a candidate has captured the primary election and represents a major party, he or she may get some help from party officials, but many candidates continue to count far more on money and support from wealthy individuals, interest groups, or their own private fortunes. They tailor their campaign themes and message to what they think local and state voters want to hear, not to the principles of the national party. Only at presidential nominating conventions does a major political party craft an official "platform"; even here, however, candidates are free to ignore it and often do. Thus, the American electorate tends not to think of political candidates as embodying general policy positions and programs; rather voters respond to the candidates' personalities, their specific promises, and their claim to be able to bring "pork barrel" benefits back to the State or Congressional district. American politicians generally win elections by getting hospitals, dams, military bases and government contracts for their district, not by running on principles.

Even in the heyday of party democracy parties were always just one element in a parallelogram of forces; they were never "conveyor belts" carrying the interests of society directly and undistorted into the highest reaches of state decision-making. Nevertheless, they were the strongest force in the political field, and the actions of their elite actors were firmly bound to the programs and images to which the parties were publicly committed and which their members battled to uphold. If the party leaders had not stuck by their proclaimed objectives, they would never have enjoyed legitimacy in the public sphere or even among the rank-and-file. Even parties without a written program could count on a widespread consensus among the party membership in support of the policies of their leaders.

In a party democracy the parties are the central force in an arena featuring a wide spectrum of other political actors capable of mediating between society and politics. They collate, focus and integrate the interests and values of a majority of community organizations, interest groups and associations, the support of which they can tap and which in turn rely on them as their strongest advocates and defenders in the political system. For example, in the Federal Republic of Germany the associations of employers, farmers, and property- and homeowners have always known that their interests were best served by the CDU. The party likewise recognized that it needed to cater to these interests in order to have a chance of winning a majority, yet it had to blend them into a more comprehensive program in order to avoid having too narrow a political base. The SPD was almost the inverse image of the CDU. It was a partner of the labor unions and tenants' associations, and, indeed, for reasons having to do with its history, it saw itself until the 1980s not simply as a partner of the trade union movement, but as its political arm.

During the entire age of party democracy, the sector of politics in which we encounter intermediary actors, among them notably the churches, has had an important function in the political process. They gave full expression to the interests and values of society, initiated and guided public discourse about how to identify problems amenable to political solution, and to choose the most promising alternatives. Furthermore, they extended their reach in many directions, including into the mass media and social forums, thus helping to shape the public realm in which parties seek majority support for their objectives. The entire network of intermediary actors has always done more than just lobby the parties. It has represented and molded a public space, in which, in the long run, participants could carry on discourses designed to produce results and could generate pressures that might gradually mobilize majorities behind potential solutions to political problems. This sort of mediating function was thus, at the same time, a way to rationalize, stabilize, and manage conflicts of interest over the long haul.

The intermediary sector

The networks, organizations and informal arbitration systems of the intermediary sector of politics are thus significant for the quality of the democratic political process not only, indeed perhaps not even primarily, because they channel interests and transmit proposed solutions to problems. Rather, their deeper importance springs from their role as forums, stabilizing factors and sources of energy for the long-term discourses about the definition of problems and alternatives for action. In the different arenas of the political public sphere as well as in the internal debates among their activists and members, they bring up overlooked themes and arguments, respond to the attacks and alternative programs of their opponents, and develop their own answers and counter-arguments in a continuing process. Groups in this sector stand very close to the people who directly and powerfully embody the problems the groups have thematized. They are thus compelled and obligated to keep their noses to the grindstone and deal with those problems, a fact which exempts them from much of the trendiness of everyday public life. In this sense they work to promote the consistency and rationality of public discourse. The description that best fits European party democracy would not so much feature independent parties competing for votes, but would instead highlight the defining role played by the intermediary sector and the parties' dependence on it. The parties may be the main actors in this sector, but they are continually and directly under the influence of expectations, arguments and pressure emanating from the intermediary organizations. The parties thus share the latter's sense of time and duration, as well as their norms of political rationality imbedded in the obligation to justify and legitimize what they are doing *vis-à-vis* well-defined interests and values.

The fact that their membership bases give political parties roots reaching deep into civil society means that interested citizens will have opportunities to take part in the formulation of political programs and to oversee the way these are implemented. In this way they represent a complete cycle of participation embracing all phases of the political process: the interpretation of interests, their integration into a program designed to promote the general welfare, the selection of personnel to advocate and implement those programs, and finally supervision of the latter's activities as officeholders and representatives charged with implementing the actions contemplated in party discourses. Ultimately it is the parties alone that have the opportunity, assuming they have succeeded in winning office, to translate their programs into official policies, and this accounts for their central position in the system of political institutions. Of course, whether the parties actually succeed in carrying out their programs depends entirely on their level of political/administrative competence. The numerous detailed functions that political science analyses have attributed to the role of parties in democratic systems can in the last analysis be boiled down to just these two.

Critics of political parties beginning with Robert Michels have always managed to uncover deficiencies in their level of internal democracy and social responsiveness, and have magnified them in public discussions.[18] Though much of this criticism is warranted, parties on the whole have succeeded in integrating state and society on the basis of mass participation, and thereby fulfilled their most crucial function. The sometimes devastating critiques of the democratic aspirations of political parties frequently overlook the fact that, even in the best case, parties can do no more than express and reflect the society in which they organize and operate. To the extent that parties intend to meet the expectation that they will provide a democratic linkage between society and state, they need an internal structure that embodies the diverse, unsynchronized, and even contradictory demands of their members. After all, the society these parties aspire to represent in electoral politics displays a wide spectrum of opinion and interest; the parties should do no less. But of course parties must always be capable of refashioning the discourses and contradictions that enliven their inner councils into task-oriented programs of action that most of their members can be counted on to support. That is after all their job as political organizations. Still, public critiques of the party system often overlook the fact that, to the degree that parties take seriously the tasks of interest articulation and integration, they can finally be no more than "parallelograms of forces" repeatedly hammering out common programs in discursive deliberations. Right-wing populists, especially, scornfully interpret as a sign of party failure an aspect that should be seen as the performance of an essential party function: integrating often contradictory social interests into a common program.

A realistic concept of parties

Derogatory terms like patronage, corruption, self-preoccupation, and gridlock have, with some justification, often dominated public debate over the role of the parties. But if we look more deeply, we find that such criticisms are aimed at the very heart of their function in a democracy. Beyond any specific services they perform for the political process, parties in a democracy have to do four things: select, delegate power to, and oversee their personnel; gradually integrate interests and values into concrete policy designs; reinterpret the tension-filled internal processes of democratic opinion-formation in light of longer-term time horizons; and participate in numerous decisions at the levels of state and society. Only in rare periods when parties are marginalized by their own leadership can a single decision-making authority centralize control over all these disparate activities. As a rule they are more likely to express the tensions, dynamics, and open-ended process-character of the parallelogram of forces emerging from the collaboration and independent-mindedness of a great number of party members at many different levels of decision-making.

Media democracy understood as the colonization of politics by the mass media fundamentally changes the role and mode of operation of political parties. To the extent that parties have to – or perhaps want to – submit to the functional imperatives of the logic of mass communication, their communicative time-frame and center of gravity shift; they respond differently to their political environment. The traditional model of a political party that reaches consensus via extended discussions with many centers of influence in civil society, that allows decisions and programs to mature gradually, and then insists that top cadres stick to them in their representational and concrete policy-making activities, has become practically an anachronism. While parties may nominally and in some aspects of their outward appearance still inhabit the public arena, their mode of operation, their substance, the game in which they are engaged have all been profoundly altered.

Summary

Democracy is not possible without a functioning political public sphere that puts the individual in a position to decide and act autonomously. The norms of democratic politics, as they are applied to pluralistic, law-governed polities, demarcate a broad spectrum of possibilities within which there is ample room for different models of democratic participation. There are three theoretical paradigms that enable us to define alternative approaches to participation in real-world politics: the model of *democracy as a marketplace*, the model of *participatory democracy*, and the model of a *democratic civil society*. All of these models are compatible with the normative claims of Western democracy. They all concur in stipulating that comprehensive, reliable information about – and drawn from – the political and social systems has to be made available.

Of course, the political public sphere involves more than just media representation; however, a democracy should still expect of the latter that it will supply appropriate political information, the key input of civic life, to the public sphere and thus promote the process of political deliberation. In this respect the logic of the political has to be considered the one indispensable standard against which the appropriateness of media representation should be measured. Political processes have a distinctive character that sets them apart from the logic inscribed in the course of processes in other systems of social action. To communicate about politics in an appropriate way means, in the first instance, to understand this logic and never to lose sight of it amid all its transformations by the mass media. This holds true no matter what level we are talking about: international relations, domestic policy, or even politics outside of formal institutions, e.g. interest groups.

In order to meet the standards of democratic politics, the mass media have to communicate political events in their own fashion, so as to bring out the characteristic features of every event they report. Thus, public communication in a democracy has to be tailored to the distinctive logic of the political process that takes place in the larger context of society, despite its characteristic method of seizing the public's attention by selective presentation and abbreviation of content. For citizens can only acquire relevant information from the media about policies that concern them if the media depict the political process in all its diverse dimensions and facets. Though the mass media never occupy the whole of the public sphere, they do help define and shape it.

Party democracy is the most prominent and widespread form of participatory democracy in Western Europe. It requires something more than reliable information about political realities: an additional public space for dialogue, deliberation, and consensus-building must be present. In a properly functioning multi-party democracy political parties are continually and directly under the influence of expectations, arguments and pressure emanating from the intermediary sector and civil society organizations. Political parties share the latter's sense of long political process time, as well as their norms of political rationality imbedded in the obligation to justify and legitimize what they are doing *vis-à-vis* well-defined interests and values. Party democracy is thus a political regime that combines deliberation and political participation.

2

The Logic of
Mass Media

Mass-media logic

In his "Critical Ideas in Television Studies" John Corner draws useful distinctions among the various forms and causes of what he calls mis-selection, misinterpretation, and misknowing, all of which he treats as potential consequences of the way viewers process television programming.[1] But he seems to assume that there is one basic form of media communication and its reception that would be free of all the distortions he analyzes. In this chapter I take issue with his conclusions by arguing that the very ways in which the media's dual filter system operate inherently tend to give a distorted representation of reality and consequently to foster "misknowing." In other words distortions crop up even when the media is functioning in routine ways. When it comes to political communications in the media, media actors must take deliberate, sophisticated measures to achieve a more balanced synthesis of media logic and the logic of actual political affairs. Only thus can they hope partially to counteract these distorting tendencies in the media. By contrast, in the case of political communications flowing through the filter system, the various "mis-" effects seem to be the most natural and obvious outcome of such mediation. Thus, misknowing and related effects are not aberrations from a putatively normal, distortion-free media presentation of politics; instead, they lie at the very heart of media communications in media democracy. Distortion *is* the norm.

As distinct from politics, the mass-media subsystem focuses public attention on a limited range of topics or themes, thereby contributing to pattern-maintenance in the whole social system.[2] Authors such as G. E. Lang and K. Lang have emphasized the fact that views of the world produced by journalists must be understood in light of a broader social process.[3] Dahlgren and, more recently, Gripsrud have pointed out that this process is imbedded in the context of the reigning forms of discourse in any age's popular culture, in this way attempting to do justice to the most successful forms of mass communication.[4] I would like to venture a step beyond their argument by examining some further issues. Just how do the media select material, and how do contemporary journalists decide the best way to present it? How do these decisions affect one another, and how much space do they leave for depicting the world of politics?

From the micro-economic standpoint, rational behavior for any individual medium means securing the largest possible market share among its target audience. From the vantage point of the media system as a whole, though, competition among individual media firms gives rise to a seemingly inexhaustible cornucopia of information and entertainment products that are meant for the public only in the sense that they were selected according to the effective demand of the target group the firm hopes to attract. Products that fail to please the targeted audience may be refined if it seems worthwhile to do so; otherwise they are simply taken off the market. Media products that present reports and information about the political world, unless they are satires, "cabaret"-style creations, or glosses that proclaim some sort of ironic relationship to political realities, must claim to have met standards of objective reporting, i.e., that they accurately represent their subject matter. The media have an extremely limited capacity to transmit a full and complete picture of the nearly limitless wealth of events that comprise political reality, so they always have to pick and choose what they will feature and how they will present it. In the best case scenario, the media's selection of stories will simultaneously pay special heed to the interests that they suppose their audience to have and to the unique features of the events about which they are reporting.[5]

Filter 1: news values

Empirical research has shown that all mass communications pass through the same filtering systems in the way they select events and emphasize certain aspects of them. This holds true of both print and broadcast media and at whatever stage of reporting, from news agencies all the way to the editor's desk. This mechanism of selection does not function as a consciously formulated, deliberately applied norm, but more in the manner of a tacit professional consensus that affects the judgments of a journalist even when he or she is not consciously and explicitly aware of its presence. It is guided by the ascribed values of news reporting that unerringly and rigorously sift through the vast range of possible choices to pick out the material most likely to capture the public's attention.[6]

The practiced eye of the media journalist, applying the standards of professional reportage in the selection process, coolly appraises each event from the real world of politics to judge whether it is really "newsworthy."[7] And this matters in the long run, because the same process of selection is applied again and again at all the various stages, so its effect is reinforced by its repeated application. First of all, the standards are applied again and again, but always with the same mindset, by each of the departments of the media system, from news agencies until the finishing touches are put on the journalistic product. Second, they influence the whole process whereby informational "raw material" gets further refined. Third, they shine the spotlight on just those aspects of the observed events that fit their expectations. The standards thus have a cumulative, repetitive, focusing quality that lends their filtering effects a nearly hermetic power. Empirical investigation of these aspects of news reporting was initiated by Johann Galtung, and, for Germany's media sciences, developed and refined especially by Winfried Schulz. In his empirical analyses Schulz identified at least a dozen factors of news-reporting and showed that they express a consensus among media actors concerning what should count as important and newsworthy.

The basic premise that influences whether or not the media will pay attention is the event character of political matters. Ideas, programs, intentions, interpretations, expectations, texts and projects that fail to qualify as events, or that cannot plausibly be honed into or at least linked up with events, have little chance of being considered as the raw materials from which the media might construct their version of reality. President George W. Bush gave a good illustration of such theatrical, contrived events in February, 2001, when he announced his new plan for massive tax cuts. Instead of simply declaring what he would ask for, Bush surrounded himself with American families of different income levels to show that all of them would profit from his plan, including those from the middle class. Of course, the families were carefully pre-selected to possess just the demographic and income characteristics that would make them the

eneficiaries of the Bush plan. Thus, a mere announcement
formed into a media event designed to silence the critics and
e public.

important factors of reportage enhance the newsworthiness of the events to be described: whatever has happened should have a short time-span and if at all possible be an already concluded episode; it should stand in close proximity to the observer, spatially, politically, and culturally; the information should have surprise value in terms of themes already introduced to and known by the audience; the events should involve conflict; and, finally, feature serious harm to somebody, or else great successes or achievements. Two quite distinct dimensions of personalization are of great relevance for all the media but are absolutely decisive for those that involve images. The media generally like to lavish attention on events that feature or are defined by individual persons, especially when the people involved are celebrities.

The more of these reportage factors that apply to an event, the higher will be its expected newsworthiness, and the more likely that the media will pay heed to it. Obviously, then, the most reliable formula for attracting media attention is to find an event with roughly the following profile: there should be a strictly limited number of prominent individuals involved who come from the audience's immediate circle, whether in a cultural, political or spatial sense, who emerge from a conflict-laden situation either with notable successes and achievements or else with grievous harm. The logic of events in the real world does not have much effect on the way the media apply these rules in selecting material to be reported. They do not wish to get involved as internal actors in the event themselves; they would much prefer simply to bid for the attention of a wide public by editing stories according to their own professional criteria. Accordingly, event and personification are the most crucial nodal points the media employ to plot reality onto their grid of coordinates.

Filter 2: the rules of stage-managing

The fragments of political reality chosen for their attention-getting value eventually end up in editing workshops, assuming they have made it through the filtering procedure dictated by the logic of selection. There they are reassembled according to another set of rules that mandate a style of presentation designed to capture the maximum attention of the target audience. This latter set of rules, as well as its skillful application to the media's finished product, is clearly affected, even more strongly than the original rules of selection, by socio-cultural trends in consumer taste and by the technical potential of the medium in question. Dahlgren, therefore, rightfully has proposed to understand modern journalism as a form of popular culture whose most prominent form is story-telling.[8] Its rules are always provisional, since they can and will be revised or scrapped as soon as they show signs of failing to win the anticipated level of attention.[9]

As might be expected, we encounter significant discrepancies in style of presentation both within one kind of medium and between media. For example, in print journalism there are clear differences between the prestige press and the tabloids, not to mention the even sharper distinctions between print and audio-visual media. Television, the formative medium of our time, has been a pace-setter, magnet and spur for all the other types. Nevertheless, one can identify a limited set of rules of presentation that cut across all media boundaries, despite differences in the final form the rules take in each case. It serves as a repertoire for determining what is possible, or commonly accepted, when the time comes to reassemble the fragments of reality selected by the filtration system. Under the influence of these rules of presentation, the media can put together a finished product that to all outward appearances faithfully mirrors some aspect of the world of politics. The system of selection that went into the report remains invisible to the viewer, so he believes he is seeing the world as it is in itself. Empirical analysis reveals that these rules of presentation are essentially the same ones used by that paragon of culture, the theater, to achieve its effects, but with a difference: the stage-management that lies behind media productions is much harder to recognize for what it is than in the theater. The way the rules are fleshed out and applied differs from one medium to another and in line with differences in the professional ethos of the media producers, but the distinctions are of degree rather than kind. Various genres from dramas and hero-tales to farce and personality story can be portrayed just as effectively in a newspaper article as in a TV show. In our own day, television's successful crusade to win the hearts of the audience has made its style of presentation into a model for the whole media system, even though the prestige print media have succeeded in keeping their distance.

Models of theatricalization

In the case of the second media filtering system, the rules of presentation, there are roughly eight different patterns that can be empirically reconstructed from a study of the way political events and discourses have been staged in print and broadcast media. They could be further refined by more careful analysis. Using terminology that sticks fairly closely to ordinary language, content analysis of political media formats for a representative day in 1997 yielded the following list: personification, conflicts of mythical heroes, drama, archetypal narratives, verbal duels, social role dramas, actions with symbolic overtones, entertainment artistry, and news-reporting rituals that promote social integration.[10]

Personification casts natural persons, by dint of the ensemble of their linguistic and non-linguistic expressions, as embodying qualities, forces, tendencies, virtues, programs or powers that carry powerful resonance in a country's political culture and mythology. Thus Tony Blair and Gerhard Schröder were cast as men of will, virtue, innovativeness and the "can-do" spirit, regardless of the actual content of the programs they stood for. And Ronald Reagan, a former movie actor, was cast as a football hero, the "Gipper," after his best-known movie role. They seem to embody more-than-human qualities that almost place them in the company of mythical heroes, far beyond what they are or ever could be as natural persons. The mythical conflict of heroes may stage the rivalry among various schools of thought, interests, and ideas in the political arena as if it were a fateful duel between heroes. The struggle between Bill Clinton and his nemesis, the Jouvert-like Kenneth Starr, comes to mind as an excellent example. On the other hand the conflict-of-heroes scenario may also inflate the political quarrels among top politicians into climactic battles between transpersonal powers of fate.

Drama and mini-drama, simple but effective templates of stage-management, are just as common in print media as on radio and TV. They depict a tragic conflict between persons, whether heroic or not, driven by fate toward a denouement that leaves behind only the victors, the vanquished, and the failures. Profound emotions about human triumph and defeat, merited and unmerited happiness and misery are presented in artistically arranged performances, dramatizing the parabolic trajectory of human existence.

We experience *archetypal narratives* in media stories featuring stereotyped, stock figures who return again and again in life and art:

the father and mother, the friend and enemy, the ruler, the good guy, the bad guy, the traitor, the innocent, the wise man, the expert, the up-and-comer, the vagabond, the sly fox, the schemer, the powerful and the powerless, all in the shape of known or unknown political actors. These figures allow the media to structure its presentation of events as a sequence of meaningful narrative episodes.

The ritual of news-reporting can be found in almost all television news formats, private and public alike. The anchorman, whether the strict and paternal or the friendly, engaging type, will always appear serious and trustworthy. At the appointed hour every day he leans forward out of the TV screen toward the assembled congregation of viewers, a familiar figure in the communal ritual of everyday life. He takes us by the hand, as he always does at this time of the day, and offers us well-measured, easily digested doses of this complicated world; he makes it comprehensible, even domesticating the mysterious and threatening aspects of it by his entertaining, calming demeanor, and inserting them into the unchanging ritual of permanent order. The master practitioners of the anchorman's art in the United States were undoubtedly the avuncular Walter Cronkite and Eric Sevareid, whom one pundit called "God in a suit."

Verbal duels are the stock recipe of one type of highly popular talk-show that knows how to capitalize at any price on conflict, intense emotion, and excitement to build up exquisite tensions in the audience. Toward that end, the moderator first picks guests who hold diametrically opposed – often extreme – positions. Then he goads the rival participants into repartee that culminates in intense confrontations, although no normal conversation, even a highly emotional one, would ever likely reach such a pitch.

The *artistry of entertainment* in politics and in its media representation is usually a harmless pastime. Fun and joking, slapstick and comedy, private stories and a bit of circus, music and games are the reasons people watch. Politicians usually go on these shows in their capacity as private citizens or "natural individuals," often with their wives and children in tow. A political topic may come up in conversation, but it will be tossed in as a side-dish and lightly touched on so as not to upset anyone's digestion or spoil the fun. Still, the forums of entertainment artistry offer politicians marvelous opportunities to prove that they have the common touch and know how to relax, as Bill Clinton proved with his saxophone.

Social role dramas, another talk-show format, take place when the guests are urged by the director to embody their social roles, say as

union representatives or entrepreneurs, politicians, critics or whatever, instead of being permitted to carry on a spontaneous conversation. The idea is to have a pre-scripted drama of idealized social roles
played out before the audience's eyes. Topics are rarely thoroughly
discussed or illuminated, and little attention is paid to real or potential actions. The moderator and cameraman instead prefer to get gestures, mimicry, and in fact all the body language of the participants
on camera, in order to deflect attention from genuine discussion of
issues. If it appears that the guests might actually reach some sort of
understanding, the directors try to get them to focus on and act out
the cliché-aspect of their social roles, which is usually not too difficult because they were invited to be on the show precisely as incumbents of those roles. The conflict of social roles that the director
assumes to be a structural feature of society is stage-managed in such
a way that the guests end up, one might say, reading from scripts
already assigned to them.

In the case of deeds fraught with symbolic significance, the deeds
and symbol-laden "acting body" of a prominent person vividly express a context of meaning with broad social ramifications by com-
pressing and heightening it into one dramatic gesture. When Willy
Brandt fell on his knees before the Warsaw Ghetto Monument, or
Ronald Reagan stood like a beacon in front of a stage-prop trench
at the North Korean border, they were acting out or proposing to the
public a certain attitude or way of interpreting events. This sort of
thing often degenerates into empty pseudo-politics, or the pure
politics of make-believe. President Reagan, for example, would pay
highly publicized visits to schools, while at the same time his administration was busy cutting school budgets. This symbolic make-
believe politics puts on an act that, for the sake of appearances,
gestures toward a real event albeit one that never actually takes place
in the real world of politics.

Aesthetics and contents

This rich repertoire of stage-management options for the media is
drawn from a stock of techniques at home in the theater. As a palette
of possibly attention-getting modes of presentation, that stock tends
to be neutral *vis-à-vis* the materials of which it avails itself. In any
given production the plot and informational content of that material
can be highlighted or downplayed. Sweeping, inexact critiques see in
the mere entertainment value of these media productions irrefutable

proof of how powerful the trend toward depoliticization really is. But a glance at the theater and a more careful look at shows drawn from the repertoire of these patterns of stage-management indicate that something else is at stake here. Of course all of the patterns have varying capacities to handle political issues, and all deal with them in different ways. But with the exception of symbol-laden pseudo-actions (admittedly a very common pattern), they can have one of two relations to the logic of politics. On the one hand, many media productions are politically disengaged, empty, and formulaic; there is nothing more to them than the entertainment value of their aesthetic forms, i.e., they are devoid of political content. On the other hand, they can sometimes be receptive to the political, seeking to transform it along aesthetic lines and using their own techniques to throw it into sharp relief through argument and information. A panel discussion on television can clarify an issue by concentrating on the give-and-take of argument and counter-argument, or it can generate pseudo-clarity. In the final analysis the show's directors care about entertainment, so what really determines viewers' reactions to what they watch are voice and gesture, carefully plotted out according to the reigning production values of the show.

There is an almost unlimited number of ways in which the aesthetics of the media can be synthesized with politics. In some cases media aesthetics can go quite far in promoting a better understanding of politics; in other cases it can be a positive hindrance. It is not so much a question of whether a show has been stage-managed, but rather of what factors enter into the production and in what manner they do this. The latter really defines how politics is transmitted by the media.

Mass-media economics

The logic of the mass media is densely interwoven with its economic structure. In the case of private media it is obvious that their products are first and foremost commodities, since sales figures are the sole justification for all of their activities, from investment to income to profits. The previous functional analysis (pages 27–35) has already shown what the media's main goal is in a general sense: capturing the audience's attention to the maximum extent possible. In the management of private media firms that goal is even more single-mindedly pursued for the sake of commercial success. Today, in the shadow of growing media concentration and competition in recent years, it has become completely out of hand. Heightened private-sector competition, especially in the boundless mass market of TV and, in its wake, the rest of the media system, has not really imposed an alien set of business-oriented rules on modes of communication characteristic of the media.[11] Instead it has led to the unchecked hypertrophy of the rules that were inherent in the media from the very outset. There is, however, a clear hierarchy of degrees to which various types of media are affected by the commodity characteristics starting from the less affected quality print media at the bottom and running up to the most affected tabloids and commercial TV stations at the top.

Mass-media markets

Mass-media markets have been seized by a merger mania in the last two decades, at least in all those parts of the world where such mergers are allowed.[12] This trend affects both the vertical and the horizontal structure of media markets. What is at stake here is not simply the effort to eliminate current and future competitors. Many mergers are designed to consolidate ownership and control of entire chains of distinct media genres in the same hands, as in the January, 2001 bid by America Online to acquire Time Warner. The strategic advantage of such mergers is clear enough: "cross promotion" of media products enables firms to exploit the entire spectrum of a product's earnings potential by engaging each single medium to promote the products of all the others. As a result the markets of the mass media, especially television, are marked by high levels of oligopoly, being dominated almost everywhere in the world by a small group of media companies. Private firms dominate the market even in countries that have large, influential public broadcasting establishments.[13]

For example, the largest media company in the world, Time Warner Inc. of the USA, earned an income of 25.37 billion German marks (roughly 12.5 billion dollars) from internally linked operations in a number of different businesses, including movies, television, cable TV, syndication, magazines, and sports teams. By the start of the twenty-first century the company was the end-result of a series of mergers that began in 1989 when Time Inc. merged with Warner Brothers, and then in 1996, now doing business as Time Warner, bought Turner Broadcasting. The largest British media company,

Reed Elsevier, earned an income of 3.3 billion dollars in 1995, mainly from a mix of businesses ranging from magazines and newspapers to book and technical presses, to data banks, fairs and exhibitions. The German company Bertelsmann AG (1995 income of 9.5 billion dollars), which ranked number two in the world, was even more widely networked by the start of the twenty-first century, earning revenues from newspapers, magazines, book and technical presses, book clubs, music publishing, sound reproduction equipment, print and industrial firms, TV, radio, movie and TV production, data transmission, online services, and trading in copyrights.

The operations of all these firms and other media giants with revenues in the billion-plus bracket transcend national and cultural boundaries. Gradually they are weighing the last anchors of regional, cultural, ideological and political loyalty, extricating their business in journalistic products from everything that might hurt sales and profits. The cardinal rule that now guides all decision-making even in the communications sector is sheer profitability, or shareholder value that is rendered absolute and freed of all social and cultural restraints. Technocratic teams of professional managers are hired to ensure that the rule is adhered to, since they recognize that the products of journalism have finally become commodities like any other, and that management alone bears a responsibility toward the shareholders to maximize their profits. There are of course individual cases that seem to deviate from the rule, such as Rupert Murdoch's conversion of his newspaper, the *Sun*, into a supporter of the Labour Party in the 1997 British election. But he could only do so because he felt certain he was swimming with the tide of public sentiment and would actually end up by boosting sales and improving the legal-political environment in which his paper had to operate. Silvio Berlusconi, the Italian media magnate, did much the same thing with his extensive media empire, using it to promote his own political candidacy in 2001, but again without hurting earnings and with the realistic hope of using political channels to improve business conditions for his enterprise.

The commodity culture

Concentration and commercialization in hotly contested media markets have tended to give all journalistic products more and more of a commodity character, since they are now typically produced and disseminated with an eye to their potential for maximizing profit.

With respect to the US McManus has documented how market forces increasingly shape the outcome of television news.[14] Media rules on capturing audience attention and thus eventually market shares dominate the business almost to the exclusion of all other principles, and are put into effect without any thought being given to democratic or cultural standards of communication.

There is a certain type of journalist who has taken advantage of this culture of commercial exploitation to fight his way to the top in private broadcast networks and in the tabloids. His main qualification for the job seems to be his readiness to pass off half-digested bits of information as sterling media products, regardless of whether he is accurately covering the issue itself and responding to its inherent standards. Business success is after all measured, when all is said and done, by ratings and not by whether one has done justice to a topic. In cases where the business interest in profit might coincide with journalistic or political goals, or when a media company has a real hope of influencing the political environment of its economic activities, media rules never exactly get suspended, but they can under certain circumstances be turned into the vehicles of explicit political messages.

Opportunity structures

The mechanism of media democracy is kept going by an interplay between institutional "opportunity factors" and cultural attitudes. Their relationship cannot be described as a closed, deterministic pattern of one-directional causation; rather, a number of powerful factors are at work here. Ratings, however, are at the heart of the system: how many sets are tuned in, the audience share, and even the number of subscribers make the whole media system dependent on ratings figures. Whether media fare gets financed or can even be justified at all, depends crucially on whether it can achieve top ratings, regardless of which media sector is involved. At the center of this system are the private television networks and stations. Their economic interests dictate that they maximize ratings for every single minute of air time, because the prices they can charge advertisers for TV spots depend on a show's ratings. Furthermore, they have to pay strict attention to the demographics of their audience, since advertisers will pay far more to put a spot in a show watched by younger viewers than they will to advertise to older ones, even if the ratings for the show are the same. Younger viewers have malleable tastes that can be molded for the rest of their presumably long lives, so they are more desirable. Private media firms, then, have a non-negotiable economic interest in maximizing the number of their viewers or readers. Their very existence hangs in the balance. This holds true regardless of what themes and formats they choose for their specific products.

The harsh economic logic to which these institutions are exposed forces them to justify all the media products they create as vehicles for attaining the largest audience, ideally of younger viewers, for that alone will ensure success in competition with their rivals. Thus, competitive pressures to maximize ratings determine most of the decisions media executives make concerning the formats of shows, how they are produced, and whether the show succeeds or is quickly pulled off the air. The most extreme case of this sort of logic can be seen in a certain practice that has turned up repeatedly in American broadcasting. The moderator of the show is kept up to date on the most current data about audience share, even as the show is going on. With that knowledge he or she can opt on the spot for whichever formats or production values are most likely to keep the ratings high. These rules are not softened even for the domains of news-reporting, political reporting and TV news magazines. Under the prevailing conditions of production, the uncompromising commitment to exploit the full economic potential of media productions takes precedence over themes, settings, the specifics of different domains of action or broadcast formats.

The pressure for ratings that afflicts commercial television is now being felt directly in legally chartered public broadcasting systems, of the type that exist in EU nations like France, Britain, and the Federal Republic of Germany. Pressure is transmitted to the public-sector systems along two complementary tracks. For one thing, it is, after all, political bodies that always have the final say on questions that affect the financial subsidies and indeed the very survival of public broadcasting. For another, the creators of media fare in the public broadcast sector see themselves as engaged in a competition for professional success with those in the private sector, and they treat high ratings as the badge of success.

The private media system has acquired a certain inertial impetus that, along with the factors just discussed, is tending to marginalize the political as a theme in the palette of formats, and to marginalize political content itself in the few remaining political offerings. The only partial exception would be the narrow sector of prestigious newspapers, but even these are continually threatened with ruin by their high operating deficits.

Media time and political time

The process that is transforming party democracy into media democracy springs from one irresistible force: the fundamental contradiction between political and media time-horizons. It results from an incompatibility between the technical possibilities and production demands of the media system, and the need for the political process to obey its own inherent and unique temporal imperatives. When the extremely short time-frame of the media's production schedule ends up dominating the public arena of politics, the result is a devaluing of those structures and organizations that are wedded by their very nature to the long time-horizon of the political process. The intermediary bodies, together with political parties themselves, are especially hard hit by these differing time-frames, which is troubling, since they are, according to the "official" theory of party democracy, the most crucial actors in the democratic process.

Political time

The political process has traditionally functioned as a series of stages. At the outset interests begin to be perceived in society; they then achieve their first formulation in the intermediary system of associations, groups, churches and community organizations; finally, political parties articulate them into broader, more comprehensive sets of alternatives, and, if they succeed in winning office, implement them in the political and administrative systems. As long as politics continues to move through these stages, it can and must follow its own inherent schedule, one which, in the case of most important issues, has typically taken years to reach fruition. This has certainly been true in Europe for important social policy decisions, including social insurance, health policy, the formula for determining old-age pensions, nuclear energy and tax policy, as well as most other matters of comparable significance. Contrary to right-wing "populist" prejudices, most such matters take time (barring emergencies that arise suddenly), and rightly so, since an extended time-horizon is appropriate in the political sphere. The latter does after all require that originally disparate positions be articulated, mediated, moved toward consensus, transformed and integrated, a process that does not simply involve the technical solution of objectively defined problems. Instead, the political process is a collective praxis, in which the overriding goals of action are set by a process of identifying common interests, persuading others, mutually transforming previous positions and giving form to inchoate interests and needs.

The praxis of the political emphasizes the participation of the largest possible number of actors and the inclusion of diverse starting-points, in order gradually to facilitate common action and the self-identification of the participants with the goals and results of the process. By contrast, solutions to technical problems can nearly always be designed and implemented by groups of experts, who are exclusively preoccupied with discovering functionally appropriate means to serve predetermined ends. The only thing that matters to the experts is the "production time" necessary first to come up with a solution, and then to put it into effect. That time can be extremely short in view of the rapid technological transformations that have been occurring, especially in the media sector. In the limiting case, given our current technological potential, it might even tend to approach zero. By contrast, as long as politics honors the inherent requirements of its own praxis, rooted in the imperatives of democracy, longer time-horizons for the political process will continue to be defensible and even essential. And this will be the case even when we do not exaggerate those imperatives by insisting that real democratic politics conform in every respect to its ideal-typical pattern.

Political time and political logic

In fact the protracted duration of political praxis is one of the most significant conditions for its success, and is therefore perfectly suited to the political sphere. Political success is not achieved by adapting means to achieve predetermined ends, but by integrating many persons and many ends, and the discursive agreements that accompany them, so as to find solutions tailored to their shared purpose. The relatively long duration of the political process in democracies has of course always run up against limits imposed by the rhythms of the electoral cycle. It should therefore not be confused with the long-term time-horizon required to plan for the political consequences of actions. Even at their zenith European party democracies had to bend to political pressure to show results by – at the latest – the end of the current electoral cycle. That meant that the dimension of the future often got short-changed when political representatives defined their horizon of responsibility and calculated the time they had left to get things accomplished. This has become a political problem to the extent that, since the 1970s, ecological thinkers have noted an ominous contradiction between the industrial-technical domination of nature, with consequences reaching far into the future, and the limited horizon of responsibility that underlies political solutions in response to it.

In economic theory this institutional dilemma goes by the general name of the principal-agent phenomenon. According to the theory, the agents (i.e., the ones receiving the task or order) always tend to seek short-term success, because they cannot assume that their principals (the order-givers) will grasp the full complexity of the cause-and-effect relationships that are involved in a given situation or that they would trust the agents to respond properly to it. The less the principals understand the details of the affairs that the agents are responsible for and manage on their behalf, the more they will seek salvation in evidence of palpable, short-term success. This is true of stockholders as well as for the average voter. Of course, to the extent that an individual takes responsibility for his or her own actions, the planning horizon for each individual will broaden accordingly, at least under conditions of sufficient external stability. Where it is a matter of providing for others, e.g., for one's family, the planning horizon may even extend beyond the individual's lifetime.

If we wish to calculate realistically the time that the political process should take, these insights suggest two limiting consequences. The first indicates that the temporal rhythm of legislative cycles imposes predictable limits on how elected political elites will calculate the time allowed them to achieve success. In European parliamentary democracies that time-frame is usually four or five years; in the United States it is only two years for the House of Representatives. The other consequence has to do with the perspective that political actors apply to the actions they have taken or might take. Do they see themselves acting as agents or delegates and thus under pressure to produce short-term results? Or are they acting at their own behest, thus primarily in civil society, the intermediary political system of associations, groups, community organizations and parties, or within their own "life-world"? In the latter case there is a greater likelihood that they will have a goal-oriented perspective on their actions, and will see the short-term success of those actions as more important than the time-frame in which they are achieved. But this goal-oriented perspective is now being applied to the very arena of intermediary political institutions – citizens' lobbies, associations, interest groups, clubs – in which the more leisurely pace and the special conditions of concerted action gave us the very template of how much time was needed for the political process to reach fruition. Still, even the time-horizons of elected political leaders in representative government do extend for several years and continue to be influenced by unrelenting pressures from the intermediary system, which has its own peculiar time constraints, dictated by its political processes, and large numbers of actors pursuing their own agendas who use and sustain those processes.

Media time

The media's schedule for its productions, by contrast, is moving asymptotically toward the magic zero-point under the influence of two internal imperatives. For one thing, the media follow certain technical rules that their experts have devised to turn out products suited to the conditions of the industry. The technical staff take for granted that their technology will keep getting better, and that they will normally have immediate worldwide, real-time distribution of their products. A photo just taken in Nepal can be seen everywhere in the world at the same time thanks to satellite communications. So much for the technical imperative. The unique economic conditions that affect media products also force them to bend to the demands of immediacy. Media products such as news reports or any other kind of novelty lose their economic "exchange value" only moments after they have been created, because the flow of the events makes them instantly obsolete, or because the virtually identical products of their numerous competitors devalue the first one, as soon as they are publicly presented.

News items about current events lose much of their value when media competitors have already long since reported them, and they become entirely worthless when they are aired again after a considerable interval. Unlike consumer or public goods, the chief product of the mass media, novelty, dissolves into thin air the moment it is presented. And by losing its use-value, it also relinquishes all commercial exchange value. The novelty that was just covered starts to get old almost as soon as the present moment fades into the past, so it is devalued as a commodity by the sheer passage of time, the emergence of a new "present moment," unless it hints that something still newer is on the way. Thus, media communications are forced into an uncompromising presentism by the structural and functional quirks of the media system itself. Its obsession with the new is not simply an unattractive by-product of the greed for profits that besets the private economy, although the latter has certainly not hesitated to push that tendency to new heights. Advances in electronic communications technology make possible this compulsion toward presentism, but the unique characteristics of the commodity called "news" make it necessary.

The media have no time; they do not even know what time is. Empirical studies have examined some of the factors in news reportage that act as a filtering system shaping the way the media perceive and construct their world. This research confirms the previous theoretical explanation for the time differential. The media take an interest in events that are both "current," i.e., going on now, and yet completed, having a definite beginning and end, such that their whole course can be surveyed and understood.[15] Only events having this temporal structure can be integrated into the media's image of reality. What interests the media in ongoing and open-ended processes is therefore not the cooperation of various actors across time, but rather the already-completed episodes in them. Thus, events that reveal their unique character only when seen and experienced as processes cannot normally be portrayed at all in the information sector of the media.

Tensions: political time and media time

One excerpt from the campaign of George W. Bush about a month before the election reveals in exemplary fashion the pattern just discussed. During a meeting with citizens he was asked a question by a woman in the audience that he had evidently not expected, and for which – just this once – his staff had not coached him to give pat answers. She asked what she should tell her friends if they wanted to know why they should vote for Bush. After long moments of confusion the candidate began offering a series of hopelessly simple-minded answers that elicited evident disappointment on the part of the questioner. Obviously, the only truly informative way to do a report of this incident would have been to display the entire process of false starts, reactions, and corrections, all of which would have taken a few minutes, as opposed to merely presenting an isolated episode from the whole sequence. However, only a few seconds were available for all of this on the evening news, just enough to show an isolated episode that could not hope to convey what was actually going on in this incident. The media only had the choice between one of the bad answers and one of the slightly better ones, either of which would just divert attention from what was really of interest in the episode.

In so far as the elite actors in the political system put their faith in the basic equation of media democracy – publicity equals success – they yield to the time-constraints of media production, because they suppose that is the price they have to pay to win public support. This is so in the trivial sense that travel, the session schedules of party conventions, events, symbolic actions, declarations, the announcements of decisions and everything else imaginable is carefully and skillfully planned for certain dates and times that seem most likely to attract media attention. Staffs of professional media experts work on these things constantly. But this ascendancy of media time over political time also holds true in a far more important sense: the time-consuming political process, along with the intermediary bodies that organize it and even including the parties, is bypassed whenever necessary in order to meet media production schedules.

The early phases of the "red-green" governing coalition in the Federal Republic of Germany (i.e., the alliance of the Social Democrats and the Greens that began in 1998) indicate what all this means in a concrete case. When the government tried in the Fall of 1998 to bring part-time employment partly under the umbrella of the country's social insurance scheme, the result was a spectacular ping-pong game of rival programs that broke out within just a few weeks. The government would present its program; the designs would be clarified and criticized in the media, then "revised" versions of the programs would immediately be offered by the government, and the whole cycle of unveiling, critique and revision would start all over again. The game continued for a total of six rounds, without any involvement from the parties, supposedly the mainstays of the government. Every attempt to include them would have wrecked the media's tight time-schedule, so it was neither seriously contemplated nor – apparently – even regretted by the participants. The intermediary system was also quietly taken out of the loop by the tempo of media schedules, while the top politicians in the executive adjusted to it in a series of breathtaking turnabouts, because they did not want to lose the chance to influence the way the media portrayed their proposals, given the long-term impact those media images would have on the public.

The uncompromising presentism inherent in the media's production time is incompatible with the time required for political processes. The core of the political is the leisurely pace of its processes with its always uncertain outcome, for which the media have no soft spot. They either reduce it all to a few tense moments supposedly revealing the "new, new thing" about it, or else they ignore it completely, save perhaps for a rare feature in a small-circulation medium for discerning tastes. The one apparent exception would be talk-shows, in which the media take the time to negotiate a middle ground between politics and entertainment. But that is only because they anticipate that the entertainment focus will make the political element palatable enough that the audience will stay tuned. The time-dimension of talk-shows is not the kind of time that distinguishes the political process; it is "stage-management" time, typical of entertainment, even when it involves political topics and actors.

Summary

As distinct from politics, the mass-media subsystem focuses public attention on a limited range of topics or themes. The media have an extremely limited capacity to transmit a full and complete picture of the nearly limitless wealth of events that comprise political reality, so they always have to pick and choose what they will feature and how they will present it.

The media apply two different filter systems in translating real events into media products. Filter 1 regulates the selection of events by applying news value-criteria: the more of these reportage factors that apply to an event, the higher will be its expected newsworthiness, and the more likely that the media will pay heed to it. Obviously then, the most reliable formula for attracting media attention is to find an event with roughly the following profile: there should be a strictly limited number of prominent individuals involved who come from the audience's immediate circle, whether in a cultural, political, or spatial sense, who emerge from a conflict-laden situation either with notable successes and achievements or else with grievous harm. The logic of events in the real world often does not have much effect on the way the media apply these rules in selecting material to be reported.

Filter 2 consists of rules of presentation. These rules are picked up from the codes of theater performance and the discourses of popular culture such as story-telling, personification, conflicts of mythical heroes, drama, archetypal narratives, verbal duels, social-role dramas, actions with symbolic overtones, entertainment artistry, and news-reporting rituals that promote social integration.

The media stage as pre-structured by the twin filters has a large capacity to handle political issues, and to deal with them in different ways. It serves as an opportunity structure for a broad variety of uses. Media productions can be successful by being politically disengaged, empty, and formulaic, i.e., little more than entertainment. On the other hand they can also be receptive to the political, seeking to transform it along aesthetic lines and using their own techniques to throw it into sharp relief through argument and information. There is an almost unlimited number of ways in which the aesthetics of the media can be synthesized with politics. In some cases media aesthetics can go quite far in promoting a better understanding of politics; in other cases it can be a positive hindrance.

The logic of the mass media is densely interwoven with its economic structure. In the case of private media it is obvious that their products are first and foremost commodities, since sales figures are the sole justification for all of their activities. Heightened private-sector competition, especially in the boundless mass market of TV and, in its wake, the rest of the media system, has led to the unchecked hypertrophy of the rules that were inherent in the media from the very outset.

There is, however, a clear hierarchy of degrees to which various types of media are affected by commodity characteristics, starting from the less affected quality print media at the bottom and running up to the most affected tabloids and commercial TV stations at the top. The pressure for ratings that afflicts commercial television is now being felt directly in legally chartered public broadcasting systems, of the type that exist in EU nations like France, Britain and the Federal Republic of Germany.

There is a sharp tension between media logic and political logic and between the uncompromising presentism inherent in the media production time and the time required for political processes. The core of the political is the leisurely pace of its process with its always uncertain outcome, for which the media have no soft spot. They either reduce it all to a few tense moments supposedly revealing the new, new thing about it, or else they ignore it completely, save perhaps for a rare feature in a small-circulation medium for discerning tastes.

3

The Process
of Colonization

Politics through the lens
of the media

According to whether one sees politics as dependent on media, the media on politics or a pattern of interdependence between them, one can speak of *theories of instrumentalization, dependency,* or *symbiosis*. Since there is little empirical support for the claim that media are functionally dependent on politics in Western democracies, we can leave aside the second model and focus on those that try to depict the influence of media on politics.[1] But taking into account the current state of media research, we can also suggest a somewhat different set of models.

The constructivist model

The constructivist model jettisons the last remnants of naive "mind as a mirror of nature" theories, whether in an epistemological or "media-logical" sense, and clears the way for the meta-theoretical insight that the media's world-views are inevitably constructed by media actors according to their own rules. We should regard this epistemological step as irreversible; nevertheless, it neglects the equally ineluctable premise that the act of constructing requires something outside itself, something that transcends the internal system that is being constructed.[2] By thus eliminating any difference in principle between the act of construction and what is being constructed, this model leaves no room for certain empirically meaningful and answer-

able questions. One might wish to know, for example, whether a construction is well or poorly suited to bringing out the inherent features
of the object being constructed. In the context of media democracy
that would mean asking whether or not media reconstructions of the
political do justice to its intrinsic character.

Fusion models

A first variant of the fusion model, by contrast, captures quite precisely the way that the political and media systems tend to overlap:
starting from the periphery, each assimilates more and more of the
other's domain.[3] But this model leads to the unrealistic conclusion
that politics must ultimately abandon its own immanent logic and
play the media's game, bending to the functional logic of media dictates. This interpretation identifies and explains convincingly a real
developmental tendency, but it takes a long step beyond what the
empirical data can support, and therefore loses a good part of its
explanatory power as applied to either domain. A second model of
fusion between the political and media spheres results from a dense
description of the way political actors behave when they enter the
media's sphere of action. It shows that the system boundaries between
the media and political worlds begin to blur when seen from the
vantage point of political actors. In so doing the second fusion model
calls into question approaches that cast media democracy as a false
front concealing fraud and manipulation. It turns out that there is
little empirical proof to support such allegations.

Fusion models also make us much more aware of new political
realities: no longer can we think of policy-making in media democracy as an activity essentially external to the way the media communicate it. Rather, policies have been internalized into the media
system and are formulated as part of a more encompassing process
of political communication. The model thus describes accurately
the tendency for political figures to "test out" or perform media trial
runs of their policy ideas prior to announcing them definitively.
Only after a variety of different tests have been run, especially on
so-called focus groups, can political actors determine which proposed policy might prove reasonably popular. So in this sense
the media help decide which policy political actors will adopt and
pursue, rather than merely communicating the latter's decisions
ex-post facto.

Comparing the models

Nevertheless, these models neglect the remaining empirical distinctions among different levels of the policy process: the image political actors project of themselves and their decisions; the way actual decisions are reached at the executive level; and the way they are implemented. Admittedly, political actors are increasingly inclined to take charge of their own media exposure, and to formulate their policy proposals in the context of focus-group testing, but there is more to politics than this. Even in media democracy the political process transcends the bipolar interplay of self-presentation and the "outside" perspective of the media. What we actually observe is a more complicated interplay among three essentially distinct levels continually interacting in complex ways, with each reflecting developments in the others. Two of these levels are located in the political system proper, where binding decisions are reached and "spin-doctors" try to assure the desired media exposure for them. The media system takes care of the public presentation of politics, and may also focus on the way political actors portray themselves, or reach decisions, or the links between those two activities. Moreover, even in media democracy media-oriented communication is by no means the only form of political communication within the system. In what one might call the "lee" of media attention, i.e., in parliamentary committees and councils, party caucuses, commissions, cabinet meetings, and executive-branch departments, a form of pragmatic political communication predominates that largely bypasses the media and focuses directly on policy proposals. Still, the participants are never going to stop worrying entirely about whether their plans will "fly" in the media.

In her broad-gaged comparative studies Pippa Norris has concluded that there is no empirical support for the most influential theories of media-malaise.[4] However, Norris's studies make no attempt to show how the mass media might contribute to an appropriate understanding of the political, regardless of the uses that various audiences might make of such contributions. This question – whether mass media discourage political engagement – would still be of considerable interest, even if the thesis proposed by Nina Eliasoph should prove valid: namely, that it is not so much mass-media communications, but instead the communications within their own life-worlds that predispose some citizens to avoid politics. Eliasoph

herself, however, mentions the theatricality of the public political discourse as one of the obstacles in the "cycle of politcal evaporation"
that prevents people from extending their political talk to the public
sphere.[5] There are two reasons for continuing to pursue the depoliticization theme. One of these is based on the plausible assumption
that the "supply side" of the mass media cannot be entirely irrelevant in shaping what the various recipients of media fare make of it.
I agree with Morley that the influence of the supply side is in fact
especially powerful on those with the least political interest.[6] Moreover, with respect to the focus of my general argument, the depoliti-
cized media rules that govern preliminary stage-management in the
political theater will in any case necessarily shape the behavior of
political actors who are trying to gain access to them. This effect does
not pertain primarily to the recipients of media fare, but to the political system itself, although it will eventually and indirectly influence
the way the public understand politics as well. This analysis will focus
on the above-described effect.

Legitimacy and the media stage

In a democracy a public sphere is and will always remain the *sine
qua non* of politics, for even when high levels of participation are not
expected or encouraged, elections still have to be held. Legitimacy,
the lifeblood of democratic politics, can be acquired only through
citizens' consent to what they perceive as the decisions made by
political elites. And the chief source of those perceptions, except in
the more personal venues of local, interest-group, and party politics,
is normally what the media choose to portray on their "stage." Access
to it, however, is conditional, given the structural stage-management
that unavoidably results from the combined operation of the rules of
selection and presentation previously analyzed. Certain political
actors hope that if they master the rules governing access to the media
stage, they can thereby increase their leverage over the way the media
present them to the public. The more diligently they strive to learn
and anticipate the rules, and the more completely they submit to them
in trying to influence their media images, the more likely that they
will end up regaining some of their lost autonomy.

The leitmotif of effective spin-control is that you can only control
the media by submitting to them. To these elites, submission appears
to be the key to securing the primary resource of their political lives:
the legitimation of power via consent. The public sphere, as shaped

by the media, therefore exerts a relentless, irresistible pressure to stage-manage politics. Those who think they can escape the ironclad rules of preliminary stage-management affecting the media are either ignored by it, or – in the best case – used as unformed raw material for the media's own productions. In this way the media tend to escape from the control of the responsible actors in the political system. This ineluctable pressure to stage-manage media events drastically alters the visible face of politics, and redraws the coordinates even of its hidden aspects.

It is of utmost importance in this context to understand that the actors of the political system play directly to the most widespread production codes of the mass media, though most of them certainly know from media research and from their own experiences that different audiences will read these messages in very different ways. From their point of view and according to their professional experience with the media, there is, however, no safer method to get their message on the media stage than by catering in the best ways they can to the basic media codes. They feel that there is no alternative to this communication strategy as they don't have other channels of access to the audiences than through the media. Thus, in this special practical perspective the otherwise mistaken identification of media discourses, audiences and publics appears to be rational. This is why politics itself becomes increasingly *politainment*[7] or a variant of *popular culture*.[8] The irony behind this is that it seems to be rational from a genuine political point of view.

Advocates of democratic theory and politics should scarcely take umbrage at the fact that politics caters to mass taste in its own self-presentation, or that it gets staged in "populist" ways. From the point when the idea of democracy as popular sovereignty began to attract widespread support, it was inevitable that politics would have to engage the mass media. In the world's oldest mass democracy, the United States, we can date media events at least from William Henry Harrison's presidential campaign of 1840, when his ward-heelers handed out miniature log cabins to emphasize his humble birth and capture the attention of the newspapers. A democracy that demanded cultural credentials for the public to vote or witness political events would be an elite club democracy, and thus none at all. The dialectic of inclusion and exclusion, of quantity and quality, forms part of the rules of the game in a democracy. Democracy always has to take into account that those most directly affected by decisions are the only judges entitled to decide what is worthy of their consent.

Critiques of this "shoe pinches" principle should be deemed legitimate and reasonable by dyed-in-the-wool democrats only if they form part of a broader effort to shape and educate public opinion. But when the time comes to reach authoritative decisions, the majority should have the final say, and judge matters as it sees them. The transformation of politics by the "mediacracy" becomes a problem if at any point the entire public can see politics only as they are seen by the broad masses (barring a major research effort on their part), and the latter have no alternative way of seeing it other than what is shown them by the media. Thus the latter end up apotheosizing the initial viewpoint of the mass audience instead of enabling them to refine and develop their inchoate impressions.

The pressure to stage-manage

The political process in all its eccentricity, with its host of actors, interests, legitimations, and alternatives, its deployment of power and influence, and its personnel and limitations still influences the way political decisions are generated in the age of media democracy. But the pressure to stage-manage politics now threatens to make the political process invisible. Before the age of enlightenment cabinet politics was a closely guarded secret; its participants, interests, constraints, and procedures were unknown even to the most attentive segment of the public, simply because the ruling elite believed that such matters were not their concern. We are witnessing something similar today, albeit for different reasons and in obedience to different rules. Because of the colonization of politics by the media system, the most decisive aspects of politics, those that directly affect the public, are moving behind the drawn shades of the media-dominated public sphere. Of course, given a pluralistic society and a diverse media landscape, this is only a well-marked tendency; there is as yet no hermetically sealed system as in the age of absolutism with its arcane cabinet politics.

Ironically enough, the motives and procedures that have brought about this fateful dualism of politics, its by now self-perpetuating fission into production and display branches, are of democratic rather than authoritarian provenance. The point has been to provide a stock of information for the vast majority of citizens that they can put to good use as they participate in political life. For the great majority of the public, politics really is exactly what it is represented to be, because it is the actions of politicians themselves, not just their reflection in the media, that have spawned so-called "media events" catering to broad mass tastes. Political elites themselves have been complicit in inducing the public to expect that the media will present a rosy picture of politics, because that favorable image will presumably help them keep their offices and mandates. The cruder the media paradigms for presenting politics become, and the more politics is depicted as a conflict of personalities, the more likely it is that politics itself will try to live up to these expectations by stage-managing its own media image. After all, it wouldn't do to disappoint or annoy the public. So politics weaves away busily on the net, in which it is gradually – much against its own will – getting ensnared.

When political actors offer insights into what they are really doing, perhaps because they feel the need to justify themselves, they are forced to admit that politics is a complex, contradictory, uncertain and open process, in which many actors take part. But, in light of the "optics" of the stage-management that has shaped its image hitherto, this honest portrait of real political processes looks more and more like a misguided deviation from what politics is "supposed" to be about. In other words, political actors are hoist by their own petard when they try to be honest, due to their long history of complicity in stage-managing their images. Now they have to stake everything on staging new media events to make up for the disappointment their momentary frankness has unavoidably caused. But for all that, the political process cannot be entirely subsumed under the rules of its depiction in the media, so public perceptions are programmed in advance to expect recurrent contradictions between the two. This is one of the causes of the public's increasing disaffection from politics. The basic principle governing politics in the media age – focusing on the present moment at the expense of discourse – makes it much more difficult for the political system to handle emergent contradictions with any prospect of success, especially in times of crisis. Usually the contradictions will be spin-controlled and given a new "look," but that just postpones the day of reckoning, which may in turn only aggravate the disaffection of ordinary citizens.

Creating obstacles for participation

On democracy's behalf, mediacracy thus invokes the democratic principles that information should be widely available and participation in decision-making as extensive as possible. As an unintended side-effect of its democratic bias, it intensifies pressures for a politics of image-making even in the political system.[9] But that is what makes it increasingly difficult for the vast majority, in whose name all this is done, to monitor and influence political events in an informed, competent way. This is the dialectic of mediacracy that contributes to a curious situation, in which we have reached the zenith of democratic decision-making potential while at the same time ordinary citizens feel detached and alienated from politics. In this respect, the dialectic of media democracy is not a closed, self-perpetuating system. When politics is made subordinate to the logic of the mass media, barriers are erected against access to the public sphere as a result of the stage-management pressures generated by the media themselves. This is a classic case of the colonization of one field of action by the rules of another functional domain of society.

The concept of colonization

Jürgen Habermas introduced and justified this notion of the colonization of one societal domain by another in the context of his theory of communicative action.[10] He wanted to invent a conceptual language to describe the conspicuous and consequential trend in which the rules of the economic and political-administrative systems increasingly dominate the life-world of modern society. The life-world has a unique origin and role: it is the one social sphere in which direct communication enables people to deliberate and reach consensus about the affairs that concern them all. Wherever differences may arise between individuals and the collectivity, be it in the neighborhood, school, community organizations and other institutions of civil society, or in the workplace or urban borough, they can be settled by conversations among those involved. In these conversations the participants have recourse to common stocks of social norms, moral rules and other taken-for-granted aspects of life that are shared by all. Proposed solutions to emerging problems can be justified or dismissed by reference to these shared norms. When a person tries to "cash in" a validity claim for his or her proposal, what counts in the life-world is solely the persuasive force of the better argument. In the processes of consensus-building in the social life-world money and power should not in principle play any role at all. Both of them are "steering mechanisms" rooted in the functional logics of other social subsystems, in this case the economic and the political-administrative, respectively. In the latter the behavior of the participants is no longer regulated by consensus, but is routed through generalized communications media. In the economic subsystem the primary medium is money, since only actual purchasing decisions will stimulate action on the part of other participants. In the political-administrative subsystem power acts as the generalized steering medium, because here decisions are implemented mainly as the result of threatened sanctions, not through appeals to others' convictions.

Since matters in the life-world that should or could have been resolved through consensus are now increasingly being decided by power and money, we are justified in speaking of the colonization of one social sphere of action by the rules of another, as a result of which the original rules are either abrogated entirely or made dependent on the second set. A classic case of this process is evident in the way that media logic has penetrated the social province of politics.

Once the sphere of politics falls under the influence of the media system, it changes considerably: it becomes dependent on the latter's rules, but without completely losing its separate identity. In colonizing politics the logic of the media system does not simply restructure the way the political is portrayed or its relation to other systems; it affects the political process at the "production" level, i.e., where the political sphere emerges as a unique form of life. The rules of media logic recast the constitutive factors in political logic, in many cases by assigning them new shades of meaning, and by adding to them new elements drawn from the media's own set of laws. Yet they never entirely succeed in absorbing the logic of politics.

Colonization in this sense thus means the almost unconditional surrender of politics – at least in all visible, publicly accessible aspects of communication – to the logic of the media system. Only in very rare and exceptional cases does the political system insist that the media should portray politics in a way suitable to the public interest. That would mean displaying its full complexity, such that the public would be in a position to judge it according to the criteria of its own functional logic. What is more, the media even rearrange the themes, procedures and relative weight assigned them in the actual process of reaching political decisions. From the very outset and in every phase of their deliberations they consider how potential themes might "play" in the media or how great their potential is to be effectively presented. Likewise, in media democracy, the resources that the involved actors and interests have to present their respective cases must be taken into account. All of these aspects are weighed as potential factors affecting the political process.

Colonization as self-mediatization

An objection that might be raised against the colonization thesis is that political elites themselves have submitted almost eagerly to the rules of the media, which regulate access to the great public stage, in order to assure themselves (in a very *political* way, for reasons of power-seeking) of having some control over the powers that decide how politics will be portrayed. This phenomenon of obliging self-abnegation does indeed occur, as critics claim. And the supposition that there is genuinely political action here, in the form of strategies for securing power, is also correct. Nevertheless, the colonization argument remains valid for three reasons. First, media pressure to stage-manage one's public image is built into the political system and cannot be avoided except in a few marginal sectors. Second, the rules of the game are established by the media system; the only flexibility left to the political system concerns how the rules will be applied. And third, in exchange for their "tactical" submission to the media rules, political actors gain a well-founded expectation that they will be invited to help shape the way the media portray them. Still, they never gain complete control over their media image. The mass media can also obey their own logic by deconstructing the self-presentations of political actors in a way that serves media interests.

Colonization by the media system has forced political organizations and institutions – including parliaments – to react by upgrading and expanding their public relations offices, endowing them with enormous resources, and staffing them with an army of media consultants who are as much masters of the journalistic craft as the journalists themselves. Working inside the political system at the behest of political interests, they know how to direct the gaze of the media toward political events and actors, such that the political reality the media encounter will have already been tailored to the interests of political elites and in line with the rules the media habitually use to construct politics.

Ways of self-mediatization of politics

Previous research has taken an overly broad and sweeping approach to the question of how the penetration of politics by the media might retroactively affect the very process and the institutional structure of politics. Various authors have noted only that mass media exert a considerable influence on the political.[11] In the following pages I intend to initiate a new stage of the discussion by showing in concrete, detailed ways how these changes come about, and what their exact nature and consequences are.

Media actors within the political system operate on two levels. As consultants they tirelessly urge the true political actors to keep the rules of the media in mind in everything they do or plan, particularly the part of it that will be publicly aired.[12] And they carefully and professionally interpret everything in their bailiwick as a rehearsal for what is to be acted out on the media stage. What observers of the media scene perceive as politics in fact has always been "mediated" in two related senses.[13] It has been jury-rigged for the mass media from the very start; moreover, it never offers an "immediate," unfiltered, direct apprehension of political reality at all. Politics has imposed this kind of double mediation on itself, so it can gain some influence over the when and how, the what and where of its media appearances.

The effects of such spin-control extend far into the policy domains in which problems are defined as political in the first place; they also shape decisions about the timing and scheduling of efforts to address them. The self-interest of political elites in spin-doctoring and control is overwhelming and permanent. It is overwhelming because media logic requires that proposals and plans simply be abandoned rather than rammed through in the teeth of bad media publicity. It is permanent because political actors are becoming ever more aware of the priority of media exposure in every phase of the political process, from issue identification in the early stages through program implementation to strategies for influencing subsequent media depictions.

We should not equate the interest of political actors in spin-control with any deliberate intention to deceive their audience, although in isolated instances that may indeed be true. Rather, there seem to be two intersecting motives at work here. First, political elites have an inescapable need for legitimacy, which feeds a permanent urge to justify themselves and their actions. Second, they are motivated to seek an edge over their rivals in the court of public opinion by cultivating a positive image. Political actors can easily justify the latter motive by thinking of themselves as good lawyers who want to use any and every means to present their clients' cases in the best possible light, but without engaging in outright lies.

Spin-doctoring

These motives for spin-doctoring are legitimate; indeed they are unavoidable in a democracy. Yet they can have harmful repercussions for the political process and undermine the respect ordinary citizens hold for their democratic institutions.[14] They may also trigger destructive collisions between the political system's long-term interests in stability and credibility, and political actors' short-term interest in gaining legitimacy by manipulating perceptions and rigging consent. The committee in the German Federal Parliament that investigated the recent affair centering on former Chancellor Helmut Kohl provides a case in point. The members of the committee were naturally the participants with the most pressing interest in clearing up the case. They quickly developed the habit of rushing out during every pause in the hearings, or at the latest by the end of the day's session, to make highly media-conscious statements before the array of cameras and microphones waiting outside. By appearing radical and uncompromising, these declarations were designed to insure the members' continuing access to the public stage. This competitive, media-oriented spin-doctoring not only weakened the effectiveness of the committee's investigation, but diminished esteem for an institution that should be highly regarded in a democratic political culture. In the end, the committee's work suffered from this loss of respect. Among political elites and the more attentive segment of the public, the suspicion deepened that the committee (as its opponents had charged) was serving partisan interests and putting on a show calculated to achieve certain public effects. The search for truth seemed to be unmasked rather quickly and thoroughly as a mere pretext for the participants to get the most effective media exposure for their own views and interpretations. In this way the Investigating Committee as an institution ran the risk of a functional implosion. While the participants were outwardly doing their work in good faith, trying to discover the truth, it became evident that what they really wanted was to produce material that would assist in their true concern, providing ammunition for a more effective media appearance.

Much the same argument could be made about the impeachment hearings in the US House of Representatives and subsequent trial in the Senate of President Clinton for making false statements and obstructing justice in the Paula Jones lawsuit case. Republicans had to make it appear that Clinton's denial of an affair with Monica Lewinsky was a "high crime and misdemeanor" worthy of impeachment, not so much because they expected to win or even believed their own rhetoric, but to satisfy their political base of religious conservatives in the South who detested Clinton. Many Democrats likewise had to "spin" the impeachment attempt as a right-wing *coup d'état*, in hopes of energizing their political base and storing up resentments for the 2000 elections. Here again, the nearly party-line votes in both chambers of Congress tended to confirm the perception that the whole thing was a partisan game, not a genuine political crisis.

Politics falls into a vicious circle under the media system's pressure to stage-manage everything. The more crudely the mass media present politics, guided by the superficial criteria they are accustomed to apply, the more politics has to call on its own cast of spin-doctors so that it does not lose all control over the way it is portrayed. By doing so, however, it plays into the hands of the media's penchant for crude stereotypes, and even confirms them, renouncing in the process the means and opportunity to show a broader public what politics is really all about.

The duplication of politics

A three-level model

Even in media democracy we can distinguish clearly three levels of politics, although the reciprocal influences and feedback loops among them have reached new levels of intensity and self-conscious management.

In the political system itself:
> Level 1   *Production* of politics: instrumental action, reaching of binding decisions.
>
> Level 2   Politics in the form of *self-representation*: self-initiated stage-management according to the media code, via the political system, of policies either already produced or not.

In the media system:
> Level 3   *Depiction* of politics from *outside the system*: politics presented *in* the media system according to its own rules.

This three-level model poses three key questions for the under-standing of politics: first, do the retroactive effects of the media system (level 3) essentially alter the logic of political action, includ-ing the factors of reciprocity affected by it (level 1), and, if so, how? Second, does the media system still accurately represent (level 3) what happens in the processes of political "production" (level 1)? And third, how does the impact of the media system affect the actual course of events in the political dimension?

The dimension of politics

Real processes of change are tied into all three dimensions of poli-tics. Analysis of the successful careers of top politicians in their contests for the leadership of their parties – such as Gerhard Schröder in Germany, Bill Clinton in the USA, Berlusconi in Italy, Putin in Russia, or Tony Blair in Great Britain – shows that their personal skills in stage-management translated into power over the media, and that this power was one of the most important, if not the decisive, resource they relied upon in their struggle to attain high office. In all Western democracies unless one has a very high, and exploitable, rank in the media's hierarchy of favor, one has no realistic chance to succeed in politics. On the other side of the coin, today a high concentration of media power or media charisma puts its beneficiary in the position to "go it alone," to act in rather high-handed ways in respect to the party's program and policies, and to focus instead on ways to conserve and increase media power. Such skilled media politicians can afford to pursue their preferred policy or abandon it, with limited regard to whether democratic discussions in their own parties had previously resulted in the contrary decision being reached.

Silvio Berlusconi's success in the Italian parliamentary elections of 2001 offers a textbook example of just this sort of trend. By going to extremes in subordinating politics to media logic, he was able to achieve political power. Not only did Berlusconi create a skillful and effective media image for himself that has had a tremendous impact given the specific situation of his country. He also set up a political party that is nothing but a media artefact in terms of its founding purpose, pre-history, and mode of operation. There is essentially no limit on Berlusconi's opportunities to guide and direct the party toward the media effects he intends to attain.

Media consultants v. party organizations

Under these circumstances decision-making power over the program and image of policies that are advocated in the name of a major party gradually shifts from the party's public councils into the inner circle of advisers around those top politicians whose power and position rest on personal, charismatic ties to the media.[15] In the wake of such a transformation the only sources of legitimation recognized as binding are poll results, expressions of opinion elicited by the media themselves (for example, radio call-in shows), and the fickle moods of the public captured at one fleeting moment in their voting decisions, themselves often just reflections of the most recent polls. Compared with stage-managed images, symbolic actions, and expressive pseudo-actions, the traditional public arenas of politics such as parties and the general public are losing ground. There are fewer opportunities for arguments to be publicly evaluated and decisions reached, while the actors who control media-based power resources amass ever more influence.

That is in fact exactly what the concept "media democracy" means: instrumental political action (the "production" side of politics) at the level of programs and substantive decision-making is, under prevailing conditions, largely disconnected from the ways politics presents itself in public. This turn of events fundamentally changes the role of one of the crucial factors in the logic of political action, namely legitimation. Personal control of media charisma that can be accumulated and strategically deployed by professionalized stage-management skills increasingly replaces democratic procedural legitimation and public discourse dedicated to educating public opinion. In this way media charisma becomes an independent and frequently dominant resource. Of course, these trends in no way imply that power has been factored out of the logic of political action. Rather, power has merely added a new resource that can compete successfully with the more traditional resources such as knowledge, competence, reliability, resoluteness, credibility, and finances.

Focus groups

Perhaps the most worrisome evidence of the media consultants' rise to prominence is the increased reliance on focus groups to fine-tune a candidate's message. There are many variations, but typically the media staff will bring together relatively homogeneous groups of 15 or 20 voters in someone's living-room, offering to pay them for their input on the candidate's speeches. The group must be homogeneous, because otherwise the participants might not be fully candid about their likes and dislikes. Media consultants want to cultivate an atmosphere of conviviality and normalcy, in which participants can relax. They are then asked to watch a taped speech and record, via an electronic device, their immediate "gut" reactions to it, indicating by various means the degree of their attraction or antipathy to the candidate's words. Additionally, the staff videotape the whole scene, carefully focusing on the viewers' facial expressions and body language at every moment of the candidate's recorded speech. They can thus eventually gage exactly which words of the speech have the strongest positive resonance with the audience and which ones turn them off. The speech is then rewritten so as to delete the unfavorably rated portions and expand, usually by repetition, parts that the focus group liked the most.

Once the specific words or themes in the speech that draw the strongest favorable responses have been identified, the candidate will be instructed to repeat them over and over again. Bill Clinton's endless evocations of the "middle class" and "hard-working families" during the 1992 and 1996 elections reflected the popularity of these slogans with the focus groups. No doubt, George W. Bush's mantra of "compassionate conservatism" had also played well with focus-group audiences. In short, focus groups substitute behavior for action, conditioned responses for rational, conscious choice, manipulation for persuasion.

On one level the focus group looks very democratic, since after all ordinary voters are having an enormous influence on what the candidate will say in his speeches and therefore what policies he will advocate on the hustings. Not only the packaging of the policy proposals, but their very substance, can be affected by the reactions of focus groups. On the other hand, the process of argument and discussion, the give-and-take of real political deliberation, has been entirely circumvented. Media consultants are not interested in why the viewers feel well disposed toward some elements of the speech and repelled by others, nor do they try to convince the participants to rethink their attitudes. Instead, they are looking for essentially irrational patterns of behavior that will help them to elicit from the voters the "proper" response: a vote for the candidate.

Politics as theater

Re-visualized culture

Our culture is being revisualized under the influence of video technology, television, and advertising; that is, we are moving away from
our previous orientation to the spoken and written word and embracing a "visual" culture of pictures and images.[16] This shift affects our
capacity to communicate in two ways. First, it immunizes certain
claims about the world as it is and ought to be against criticism by
virtue of the suggestive power inherent in the images' effects on the
viewers. The members of the audience are subtly urged to take their
first, immediate perceptions at face value, and not look beyond them
to see how and why they arose. In that way, the images paralyze our
critical faculties. At the same time the new media restrict the traditional culture of discourse to the public stage. This aestheticizing
of the political public sphere is a response to the prior stage-
management of electronic media forums, as well as to the way the
faculty of social judgment has been touched by the new visual culture.
Political communication lost no time in taking advantage of the shift
toward visualization in forms of communication and experience
brought about by the dominance of television. Politics is portrayed
in the media more and more often – and masterfully – as a sequence
of images and media events. These mediated events are dreamed up
by advertising and communications experts and fine-tuned by the
actors to guarantee maximum media exposure. Their core elements
are a series of gestures and symbols, episodes and scenes, images and
stage-sets: in short, messages of all kinds borne by images rather than
discourse.[17] On the media front, the culture of the image privileges
media productions that lend themselves to visualization. On the political side it encourages the staging of "politics for show," replete with
imagery. In the latter case the public cannot always tell right away
whether it is seeing political artefacts depicted with advertising
acumen, or whether the media events are the sum total of the
political "production." Politics tends to become politainment, a vivid,
scintillating show.

The electronic stage generates an aestheticized politics based on
obliging communicative habits in the life-world.[18] It molds the citizens'
powers of judgment by the strategic exploitation of their perceptions,
and tends to care very little whether all these images are ever backed up

by political action or not. Under these circumstances a considerable part of the energies, intelligence, and planning in the political sphere is devoted to fabricating a semblance of political action.[19] The latter replaces information, interpretation and discourse by efficaciously staged visual impressions and calculated manipulation of images. Television and those who create its images are deeply implicated in a re-visualized culture, which they both serve and sustain.

Performing theater

Edelman has shown that not only political reportage in the mass media, but even political events themselves always display both instrumental and symbolic-interpretative aspects.[20] Subsequently I would like to investigate the relationship between these two elements. I am particularly interested in the aesthetical forms of symbolic politics, the criteria governing how boundaries are drawn between the latter and the policy dimension. I would also like to ask what conditions must be met in order for the relationship between these dimensions to be seen as proper.

The theatrical approach to the display of self and politics seems almost ready-made for the media stage.[21] Such displays convey their messages in four closely related, cross-referenced dimensions: *stage-management*, *embodiment*, *performance*, and *perception*.[22] The point is always to generate premeditated meanings in the minds of an imagined public through the performances of a body in action. The latter brings to bear not merely the meaning of the spoken language, but all the semiotic systems of which it is capable: mimesis, gesture, paralinguistics, proxemics (body language), props and stage-sets. In the traditional artistic theater the densely woven illusions that arise in this way are recognized for what they are, i.e., as simulacra of the real world; thus, they trigger aesthetic and social insight. In the media and politics, by contrast, they conceal, either inherently or by means of well-orchestrated efforts, their staged character, and so they create the illusion that they are reality. Like any staged production they could evoke the reality that underlies them by aesthetic devices, but in fact they generate semblances whose reference to any real-world equivalent save the calculated stage-management of their authors remains always an open question.

Politics as theater has three basic staging strategies available for the mass-media stage: pseudo-events, image projections, and pseudo-actions.

The politics of the media event

The notion of the pseudo-event has been common currency in media studies since the 1960s.[23] Ever since the early days of the media age it has been an obvious move to deliberately stage occurrences or messages whose event-character would give them outstanding news value. The politically staged pseudo-event, which we now routinely call a "media event," was one of the first instances in which the world of politics kowtowed before the laws of the media. Nowadays every local reporter, not to mention any reasonably aware citizen, understands that citizens' complaints and demands have to be dramatized to get attention. For example, if citizens merely propose that pedestrian stripes be painted on a street corner to make crossing the street safer, their proposal will likely be ignored. If, however, they should block off the street and paint their own temporary stripes to gain attention, that will probably be reported as a newsworthy event. The boundaries are never sharply defined between obvious pseudo-events and those that can successfully conceal their pseudo character. And the repertoire of options for stage-managing pseudo-events is practically limitless.

Staffs of media consultants working in the political system not only know that they have to stage events (and non-events as well) according to media rules in order to secure front-page headlines for them and give them global significance.[24] They likewise have mastered the rich palette of theatrical stage-management options. They bow to the requirements of the media by packaging their wares in a highly professional way or delivering well-packaged but innocuous "showpieces." At that point the media could, if they wanted to, simply pass on to the public the original version of the pseudo-event that had been handed them, persuading themselves that they would be reporting something that had actually happened in the real world. Alternatively, they could analyze the stage-management behind it to ferret out its real content, but that involves competence, time, and work, and runs the risk of incurring the displeasure of the politicians whose media events had been picked apart by the pundits. There is thus a tendency for the media rules and the political interest in favorable publicity to merge into one single syndrome. This is, however, no more than a widespread cultural practise in making use of the opportunity structures inherent in the pre-production of media stage. The option to make use of them in different, more responsible and sophisticated ways is always open.

Among the media advisers' favorite pseudo-events are tree-planting, holding press conferences, making visits to gather "first-hand" information (especially when there has been a flood, fire or some other disaster), and laying corner-stones, which may involve the politician actually picking up a shovel. In the case of the pseudo-event known as a "dedication," the dedicating politician is promoted to the rank of "father of the new," on account of the profound mythological resonance of what he is doing. Even retrospective pseudo-events like jubilees and commemorations can create similar effects. The joint appearance of Clinton and Kohl at the 50th anniversary of the Berlin airlift in May, 1998 was staged in such a way as to make them seem like honorary co-heroes, latter-day embodiments of the heroic spirit of those days. More recently, former President George H. Bush and US Secretary of State Colin Powell turned up in Kuwait to celebrate the tenth anniversary of the Gulf War, and incidentally to build a symbolic bridge of continuity between the new Bush administration and the most popular achievement of the old one. One more recent example of this kind of symbolic politics was staged by the George W. Bush government in the wake of the 11 September 2001 events. As soon as the President had declared the new war against terrorism, but was not yet able to satisfy the nation with pictures of real action, his cabinet members several times presented themselves to the media in kind of military uniforms to create the impression that they were indeed in the middle of the new war already.

The politics of image

Image is a pseudo-event in the domain of ethics, pseudo-action as personification. The historian Daniel Boorstin put that insight on record back in the 1960s when media democracy was just getting under way in the United States. The term image refers to a staged artificial product consisting of carefully designed pseudo-actions, in which a natural person is presented as the personification of qualities highly esteemed in the mythology or ethics of his or her commonwealth. Polling organizations ask voters even at the stage of primary elections which qualities they value most in their leaders: trustworthiness or energy, likability or a sense of responsibility, honesty or the ability to get things done. With the results in hand, media advisers script strategies for public appearances and pseudo-events, gestures and settings capable of transferring the desired qualities into the media image of the candidate, provided of course that these are compatible with the person's natural characteristics. More significant than all these details is the overall impression made by the candidate and his or her proximity to archetypical heroic figures endemic to the country's culture. Jacques Chirac, for example, could never wear the cowboy boots that Bill Clinton gave him as a gift, at least not without causing a political disaster in France, whereas George W. Bush could wear them and warm the hearts of his countrymen, at least those from the West.

Still, media advisers can modify the candidates' natural characteristics to some degree in order to make their embodiment of the ideals to be portrayed on the media stage more believable. Qualities can be expanded or reconstructed, emphasized or downplayed, exaggerated or minimized as circumstances dictate. The media experts devise a mosaic of images and poses, encounters and situations, episodes and stage-sets, that come together in pseudo-events to form a composite picture of the candidate as the public is supposed to envision him. The hero as a peer among this world's heroes; the hero talking to the old and feeble; the hero as conqueror of hordes of opponents in his own camp. The bodily image of tranquility, energy, determination, and equanimity. The divine wrath of the just man. The confidant of corporate executives, artists, and media stars.

The main theatrical strategy of the politics of image is a kind of role confusion typical of the stage. The images that are supposed to make good the candidates' claims to personify desired qualities, and so enhance their credibility, allegedly come from "natural" situations that have not been contrived for public effect. We were taught to think of Ronald Reagan as a down-to-earth, folksy President, because we watched him chop wood at his ranch. The lenses of distant cameras were never allowed to get too close, precisely to avoid the impression that his wood-chopping was a media event and not something he would have been doing in any case. The combination of image and pseudo-event in scripted episodes that are physically acted out is the scenario of symbolic pseudo-politics.

Symbolic pseudo-politics

The classic case of this brand of media-oriented politics, repeated in countless variations almost everywhere, is often manifested when politicians make their appearance, and the TV cameras are rolling. President Reagan, in one particularly outrageous instance, once sat on a bench in a school classroom apparently engrossed in conversation with the teachers and pupils. He was providing a stage-managed demonstration of his allegedly great interest in the country's educational system for the eye of the beholder, while behind the scenes he had in fact just drastically cut the education budget. The political actor plays his scripted role in the episode, making the most of the full range of theatrical possibilities, as if to suggest that he is actually carrying out the role assigned him, when in truth nothing happens at all. This sort of symbolic politics is placebo politics, acting out some role for the purposes of make-believe. We encounter it in all of those instances, more and more frequent, in which staged images counterfeit and thus displace real-world actions, substituting make-believe for real political change. The dedication of factories and meetings of interest-group representatives, business leaders, and scientists are two of the most popular episodes designed to generate symbolic placebo effects.

Symbolic politics showcases theatrical pseudo-actions that, unlike genuine symbols, do not offer a denser, more authentically experienced slice of reality, but instead lack any reference to reality at all. Consequently, we may think of symbolic politics as strategic action offering no arguments and establishing no real connection between its aesthetic semblance and the essential reality toward which it points. And yet its semblance suggests the existence of just such a connection through images and sense-impressions conveyed by the body in action, rather than through any discursive claims about it. An episode in the scripted narrative is acted out as though the actor were doing something in the real world, so that the distinction between play-acting and reality is effaced.

Symbolic politics old and new

The essence of symbolic politics today, as distinguished from its role in earlier stages of history, lies in the way it combines a democratic pattern of legitimation, techniques of visual communication, and politics as a star system.[25] Taken together, these elements fundamentally alter its potential and actual existence. Techniques of persuasion work even in democracies that lack a single figure at the top who embodies the state and in which therefore a multitude of "star-quality" political actors are forced to share the limelight. State-of-the-art visual techniques have become so sophisticated that they can reduce the amount of "talk" in persuasion down to a subordinate vestigial remnant. The real work is done by personifications and their pictorial representation. The function of symbolic staging has changed fundamentally, and its possibilities have been brought to perfection in unparalleled ways. Under cover of banal but pleasant entertainment, a new type of strategic communication has made itself at home.

As M. Edelman has argued, political action has always had an aspect of expressive symbolism; without that, the commonwealth would not hold together.[26] Every law, besides its explicit purpose, is also meant to evoke the underlying norms of the society it regulates. Laws that purport to punish behavior a society cannot in practice prevent are nothing but symbolic politics, but that is not always necessarily a bad thing. Decrees, speeches, and actions can all be forms of symbolic expression. And if they do not spread deception in their design or effects, but rather focus attention, evoke shared commitments, and spur people to act, then they are a legitimate and often productive political tool, provided they do not usurp the place of discursive legitimation.

Summary

As democratic politics is dependent on legitimacy through continuous public support, politicians have a vital interest in a sufficiently frequent presence on the media stage. Access to it, however, is conditional, given the structural stage-management that unavoidably results from the combined operation of the rules of selection and presentation previously analyzed. Thus, politicians feel themselves to be under ceaseless pressure to stage-manage in order to get access to the media. They hope that if they master the rules governing access to the media stage, they can thereby increase their leverage over the way the media present them to the public. The more diligently they strive to learn and anticipate the rules, and the more completely they submit to them in trying to influence their media images, the more likely they will end up regaining some of their lost autonomy. Consequently, the sphere of politics falls under the influence of the media system.

According to J. Habermas the colonization of one societal domain by another happens when the first succeeds in imposing its own specific rules on the latter's way of functioning. As the sphere of politics falls under the influence of the media system, it changes considerably. Colonization in this sense means the almost unconditional surrender of politics – at least in all visible, publicly accessible aspects of communication – to the logic of the media system. Political actors are becoming ever more aware of the priority of media exposure in every phase of the political process, from issue identification in the early stages through program implementation to strategies for influencing subsequent media depictions.

As a result of these changes politics becomes at all levels dependent on the media rules, but without completely losing its separate identity. Even in media democracy we can still distinguish clearly three levels of politics: the *production* of politics; politics in the form of *self-representation*; and the *depiction* of politics *in* the media system, although the reciprocal influences and feedback-loops among them have reached new levels of intensity and self-conscious management.

The key resource for the political system to manage its access to the media stage lies in the theatricalization of its own performance. The theatrical approach to the display of self and politics seems almost ready-made for the media stage. Such displays convey their messages in four closely related, cross-referenced dimensions: *stage-management*, *embodiment*, *performance*, and *perception*.

The point with theatricalization is always to generate premeditated meanings in the minds of an imagined public through the performances of a body in action. The latter brings to bear not merely the meaning of the spoken language, but all the semiotic systems of which it is capable: mimesis, gesture, paralinguistics, proxemics (body language), props and stage sets. In the media and politics theater-like presentations tend to create the illusion that they are reality. Politics as theater has three basic staging-strategies available for the mass-media stage: pseudo-events, image projections, and pseudo-actions. All of them are used with increasing professionalism and frequency.

It is of utmost importance in this context to understand that the actors of the political system play directly to the most widespread production codes of the mass media, though most of them certainly know from media research and from their own experiences that different audiences will read these messages in very different ways. From their point of view and according to their professional experience with the media, there is, however, no safer way to get their message on the media stage than by catering in the best ways they can to the basic media codes.

4

The Effects
of Colonization

The persistence of the political

Communication culture

Despite these tendencies there is no question that the logic of political processes continues to define political competition, even as the influence of media logic keeps spreading.[1] Conflicts over competing policies, whether pursued by parties relying on persuasion to get their program through parliament or by the media strategies of top-level actors, still follow the established patterns of the political process. Actors pursue interests, even when the media dominate the circumstances under which they act. They wield various power resources, among which the availability of the mass media play a new and crucial role. And they use social, economic, and media power to shape events. In other words, although the inherent logic of political action may indeed be modified, supplemented, or accentuated in new ways in the course of a political process now thoroughly dominated by the logic of the media, the latter will never entirely displace or absorb political logic.

The dimension of polity

Traditional political analysis treats the constitution and political culture together as the framework that defines the parameters of action for the commonwealth. But media democracy has presided over the emergence of a "constitution" and communicative culture rooted in the media system which have partly supplemented and

partly redefined the older institutional framework. Of decisive importance in this context is the role of tabloids versus high-quality print
or broadcast media as well as the structure of control behind both
sectors. They define the way politics is communicated to a wider audience and thus the conditions under which political logic and media
logic are synthesized, and how media charisma may be accumulated
by elite actors. Moreover, the manner in which actors inside the
media system handle the logic of the media also helps to distinguish
the respective communicative cultures of different societies. This
pattern cuts across the previously described influences of media types
and structures of control. Media logic potentially grants actors a
great deal of discretion in deciding upon suitable ways to portray
politics in the media. Communicative culture, as one aspect of the
broader political culture, has a chance to pre-define what will count
as adequate political information for the citizens and thus to set the
conditions for their civic roles. Here again the commercial broadcast
networks and stations play a dominant role within the media's
"constitution" on account of the unrelenting pressure they exert for
broadcasters to boost audience shares and ratings. The communicative culture and media constitution are thus becoming integral components of the broader constitution of the commonwealth. And they
radiate outward to affect the role and substance of political culture
and communication as well as the quality of democratic politics and
oversight.

The dimension of policy

When the media system colonizes its political counterpart, it multiplies and heightens opportunities for symbolic pseudo-politics and
stage-management for dramatic effect. Sometimes, the latter may
entirely replace real programs of political action; in other instances
pseudo elements may be blended into a depiction of real political
practices.[2] These opportunities are exploited imaginatively and often,
especially when political channels start to become clogged. The pressure on nation-states to acquire legitimacy for prospective political
action or even inaction grows considerably, when – as for many
European countries today – they are touched by economic difficul-
ties. The pressures are intensified if the causes of such economic
problems, in this case globalization, defy the power of individual
countries to respond effectively to them. This helps explain why political actors increasingly feel tempted to conceal their obvious failures

behind high-profile pseudo-events that play to the media. Opportunities for such legerdemain are extensive, since the average citizen has little basis for judging political action except by observing what is happening on the political stage. For average citizens it has become difficult if not impossible to examine critically, say, the Prime Minister's lavishly staged ribbon-cutting ceremony for the opening of a new factory. They cannot really say whether the whole scenario was politically inspired, whether the political dealings behind it might contribute to improving or worsening the balance-sheet of job-creation, or what might be deduced from it about behind-the-scenes rivalries among different actors. Many of the latter count on the same tried-and-true recipe for success: stage media events that show off your achievements and burnish your image.

Symbolic pseudo-politics

At the level of problem definition, citizens may indeed still have the opportunity to cross-check what is said and done against their own independent life-world experiences. But that is becoming far less true for the adroitly stage-managed, symbolic pseudo-politics and image-making we have been discussing. Only at the end of a complex, nearly impenetrable process, do the unresolved problems come back to haunt the life-world of the affected public. Despite the glossy media images, few can overlook the consequences for their lives of unemployment and violence, social degradation and environmental damage. So even in the world of stage-managed politics, the public has to fall back on the traditional political questions as its final criterion of judgment: what programs of action have been adopted, and have they actually succeeded? Even in media democracy everyday discourse about one's own experiences with the political system remains the ultimate, uncompromising criterion for judging politics and politicians. Thus, strictly speaking, within the domain of politics every single dimension of the logic of the political may indeed be overlaid, supplemented, refashioned and relativized by these new, media-oriented factors of stage-management, but old-fashioned politics is never fully eclipsed.

The political process allows the cards that determine the power and career opportunities of the political stars to be reshuffled and redealt, but the actors and their power resources dominate the whole proceeding. The commonwealth's constitution changes under the influence of the media system and its communicative culture, but political culture and institutions continue to function as the framework and conditions of political action. It is certainly true that staged pseudo-politics has spread like a weed and that programs of political action are increasingly virtuoso performances played to the audience. Yet the question of whether political programs have really worked never quite pales into insignificance under the blinding klieg lights of media attention; in fact the traditional questions reassert themselves when we are faced with the experience of crises in our everyday lives.

During parliamentary or Congressional committee mark-up sessions on a given bill, most participants are initially interested in finding the best objective solution to a problem. In the open negotiating sessions they can generally rely on one another not to use internal arguments and log-rolling offers as ammunition in the media phase of their political conflicts. But the participants never quite forget that the way the whole project may be portrayed and communicated in the media, especially in respect to the weaknesses of their opponents' position, is an issue lurking in the communicative background of their negotiations. In civil society's community organizations and town meetings matters are frequently debated with an eye to reaching consensus, or at least according to the formal principles of fair negotiation. But even here discourses often follow media communications and show an implicit awareness that the participants may eventually appeal to the media's wider audience to solicit action from the politicians. The only partial exception would be those cases in which political initiatives emerging from civil society and the lifeworld would result in proposals that can be implemented only at the local level, although even here media publicity still influences political strategies to some extent.

Despite all these qualifications, the preeminent fact concerning political communication in media democracy remains the colonization of politics by the mass media. Even the portion of political communication that is not directly media-related still takes place within the horizon of communicative rules at work in the media. And the much greater part, the one concerned with the public legitimation of political action, is by its very nature wedded to these media rules. For these reasons the model of media democracy advocated here may not describe the whole of communication under these novel circumstances, but it depicts a characteristic and crucial part of it.

Politics as popular culture

How media actors
justify theatricalization

As Morley has demonstrated, under the influence of its given cultural environment and the basic rules of the media logic journalism itself becomes more and more part of the popular culture of its time.[3] This tendency to mix different types of discourses with regard to their most succcessful popular forms prevails in all parts of the media system. In this respect there is a continuum rather than a gap between quality media, tabloids, and popular television. In all of them the dominance of the aesthetics of popular culture may serve either professional journalistic ends or exclusively entertainment interests, or a variety of types of mixtures between both of them. Consequently, in the course of the colonization of the political system by the rules of the media discourses, a substantial part of politics proper tends to follow the same trend. To that degree politics itself becomes politainment, a form of popular culture.[4]

As examples of the way in which these processes may also serve to infantilize politics, we can point to several actors famous for their trivial roles who rose to political prominence at the end of the twentieth century by transferring their immature personas into the genre of politics and using their fans as a ready-made electoral base. The belief has gained currency that political parties are first and foremost bureaucratic organizations staffed by career officials trying to promote their own interests at the expense of those of society at large. Media actors, including journalists, editors, and executives, have often accepted that diagnosis and judged that the transition from party to media democracy represented a positive step for democratic values. This idea has been advanced in a variety of forms, all of which assume that less party influence equals more democracy.

What tacitly underlies all versions of the argument is the conviction that media-oriented populism is the most direct route to democracy. The German journalist Dirk Kurbjuweit, a critic of traditional party politics and admirer of the theatricalization of politics, has tried to demonstrate this thesis as vividly as possible through carefully drawn portraits of two actor-politicians, Jesse Ventura and Josef Estrada.[5] By virtue of their superior skill as performers, now almost second-nature in both of them, these former showmen are now "the only politicians who could become popular without the machinery of a party." Undoubtedly, almost all the politicians who try their hand at the performing arts on the media stage, either on their own behalf or for the sake of a cause they advocate, come up a bit short. But these two actor-politicians are said to embody a truly democratic alternative to the media-honed acting talents of professional politicians, in spite of the playful way they take center stage, and the apparent randomness of their political practice. Of course, Estrada's media charisma did not save him from being removed from the presidency of the Philippines on corruption charges. But the mere fact that he even made it that far in politics would prove to Kurbjuweit that actor-politicians have the inside track in democratic politics.

Borderline cases: Ventura and Estrada

In contrast to professional party politicians, both Ventura and Estrada were almost destined to be "men of the people," because they lived colorful, eventful lives that had already brought them into every nook and cranny of society, and allowed them to see it as it really is. They could be so sure of the effectiveness of their stage demeanor that they did not even have to act in their new political roles any longer; they could just "be themselves" without worrying or calculating what sort of impression they would make on others. Their talents as performers had bestowed great success on them long before they made up their minds to use those abilities as a springboard into political careers. In this sense they exemplify what Kurbjuweit calls the principle of "body politics" as opposed to "briefcase politics." The latter is the style of the traditional type of politician, who devotes his time to the study of texts, administrative documents, working papers, and talking-points for negotiations, all "fodder for the tedium and arduousness of traditional politics: its bureaucratic, non-sensuous, and thus inhuman dimension."[6] In contrast to all that, the body politician counts on his immediate physicality and its hold on the media. It is as though he were projecting a media-ready astral body, and the public, grateful not to be bored by any arguments or factual information, shows its enthusiasm for the sheer entertainment value of his appearance. The actor-politician is so self-assured he could almost do his routines in his sleep. Effortlessly playing Mr Honesty, he is a smash hit.

The actor-politician does not have to gain the consent of any political organizations in order to display and prove his talents as a performing artist. On the contrary, he transfers his sheer charisma as a performer, well tested in the pitiless glare of show business, directly into the arena of politics, which means that he does not have to depend on anything or anyone else except his own talent as a performer. He owes nothing to any lobby, association, interest group or party, as long as the media aura of his public body lasts. Assuming that politics will always verge on political theater in our media society anyhow, albeit a second-rate theater given the semi-skilled nature of the political actors and their indebtedness to organized interests, then why not take the easy road and opt for the democratic play of the true actors? But they are not only actors, for they live right in the middle of society as "different" politicians in all their spontaneity and independence. And both of these "alternative politicians" do have their own political programs. To be sure, these have very few details, commitments, specific plans of action or reasoned justifications of their positions, of the sort typical of establishment "briefcase politics"; nevertheless, they convey a significant political message. Ventura told *Playboy* that, "he was conservative in fiscal policy, liberal in social policy, wanted to develop the world's best educational system in Minnesota, and that religion is something for weak minds."[7]

Fortunately, argues this journalist, neither man has ever seen the inside of a political party. One enters these grinding machines early and gets ground down to the proper shape. But actor-politicians, free from all the petty details of accountability and participation by other people, do not shrink from even the most monumental tasks: "abolishing the Senate, building trolley lines for the auto-addicted, making quantum leaps in the educational system."[8] One political scientist from the University of Minnesota complained of Ventura that the actor-politician might lack respect for the institutions of government, because he never showed up in the State Legislature. But the journalist concluded from her looks ("her hair is short, she has thick glasses") that she must be a media society pansy, whose criticisms simply reflected the resentment of a loser.

Kurbjuweit has unintentionally brought to light the truth about media society. If democracy is nothing but legitimation by the most successful form of communication, then the communications artist is the best democrat, with no effort whatsoever. And if the authentic play of body politics is the most efficacious form of entertaining communication, then "briefcase politics" with its institutionalized procedures and long-winded arguments might as well bow out now. But one caveat is in order: boom times are the precondition for body-politics. When the economy is humming along and no war threatens, citizens like the kind of politician who lacks expertise in the business of politics, as long as he is entertaining. But then again, they think, the body-politicians should not be allowed to get too close to nuclear weapons and such, nor should they be involved in staff meetings when there is a real crisis looming.

> In a crisis people have more confidence in the old-fashioned briefcase politics. But at the state level, where it is more a matter of repre-sentation and mood, I would opt for Ventura and his advisers over someone like the staff and governor of North Rhine-Westphalia, Kurt Beck, who is a good-natured fellow with a full beard. (Kurbjuweit: 2000, p. 34)

New plebiscitary democracy?

The interest that media-entertainment policy evinces in being seen as politically legitimate is something more than an ironic game. Nor does it spring simply from the annoyance media professionals feel when they see how inadequately many politicians stage-manage their own appearances ("these political amateurs are always ready to play the media game; unfortunately, they're not very good at it"[9]). Rather, their interest is an attempt to uncover an element of plebi-scitary democracy in the convergence between the vital need for entertainment that most people feel and the media stars' talent for providing it. In their view, the emotional connection that springs up between audience and stars is far superior to the indirect and formal relationships inherent in democratic procedures and institu-tions. This self-serving brief in favor of entertainment as democracy conceals a radical misunderstanding about the role of the political in democratic communication. And that is an even more serious defect than its tendency to disparage old-fashioned politics, i.e., the gradual process of interest-aggregation, institutional oversight, par-ticipatory decision-making, consensus-building through argument and counter-argument, and the continuity fostered by intermediate organizations.

Entertainment, rationality and information

We must never lose sight of the fact that communication cannot fulfill its political function of democratic legitimation unless it maintains a nucleus of rationality, discussion, and reliable information; unless it is subject to argumentative accountability and capable of generating consensus. This holds true even in the media age, however much communication may have come to resemble entertainment in its quest for a wider audience. If this rational core should ever disappear from communication, it would no longer be political in the sense of promoting democratic legitimation and control, no matter how much more exciting the "plebiscites" of entertainment artists were than anything normal politics had to offer, and regardless of how widely diffused their messages might be. Democracy reduced to sheer entertainment ceases to be democracy. Democracy can never solely be a matter of communicative accord between public actors and their mass public; rather it involves consensus-oriented deliberation and its continuing revision. In principle politics *qua* entertainment can never be made fully accountable, nor even convey any notion of political realities, because there simply is no politics going on behind the stage and no slice of political life is being analyzed.

The purveyors of political entertainment love to focus on the "personal" side of politics, especially the all-too-human weaknesses of political actors. Indeed, success stories in policy-making are always portrayed as lucky hits, while corruption is declared to be the nature of the system. Politicians are depicted as having been led astray by the will o' the wisp of fame, and all boundaries among law, morality, and order become fluid. The definitive legitimation for these shows appears to be the idea that the mass public wants them to be staged. Anything seems possible, because one can make a play out of anything and sell it to the media public attuned to "trivial" entertainment genres. The boundaries between fantasy and reality begin to blur, as they do for small children. The psychological law driving this sort of boundary-effacement is infantilism.

It must be underlined, however, that the journalistic and political discourses about political reality, however stage-managed they may be, invariably do make implicit claims to authenticity and rationality. Within broad limits they indeed permit information to be adduced concerning political issues, and, to a lesser extent, feature the repartee of argument and counter-argument. Furthermore, there is no reason to doubt that the media can provide complete, accurate information while at the same time indulging in various degrees and kinds of stage-management. The two activities are not mutually exclusive. We might suggest a comparison between media productions of politics and pedagogy. Neither the simplifications nor the trivialization automatically devoids media or political discourses of all content.

Certain forms of media-staging may likewise produce a synthesis that transforms the subject-matter without compromising the integrity of its informational core. Infotainment is not the enemy of information *per se*. In the light of recent media research an a priori separation between informing and entertaining discourses is not justified, notwithstanding the experience that stage-managed discourses in the media and in politics are in fact frequently issueless.[10] However, the media's commitment to entertainment, drama, and emotional involvement may open up access routes to the domain of political affairs that would otherwise remain closed to many people. After all, attracting attention to themes of common interest and presenting them accurately is precisely the social function of the mass media. The question that has stirred the most critical comment from partisans of democratic politics is whether the mass media's attention-getting devices enthrall the audience at the price of distorting the essential reality of what they are trying to present, folding it into a stage-managed simulacrum. The temptation to do this resides in the opportunity structure of the media system itself, since as a rule the mass public will tolerate attractively staged productions, even if they are practically devoid of content.

Remote control culture

Television languishes under the tyranny of the remote control. Every new scene in every show or commercial is designed to prevent the viewer from switching the channel. This constraint alone gives strong impetus to the tendency toward infantile media content, just as happens with children's shows: every moment has to count, in order to accommodate the audience's short attention-span. The constraint of having to keep the greatest possible number of viewers tuned in leads many show producers to feature as many loud sound-effects as they can squeeze in. After all, even short periods in which viewers tune-out can cost a station or network a great deal of money. The media feel relentless pressure to serve the broadest possible mass taste, and they are always trying to expand their viewer base, or at least hold onto what they have against tough competition, by increasing the dosage of trivia and spectacle in their shows. These trends conspire to cause a relentless "dumbing down" of the cultural and political quality of TV fare. Public broadcasting does not labor under such intense pressures, partly because it is accountable to the public, and partly for reasons of journalistic ambition. However, the same tendencies are at work even there, due to their perceived need to keep pace with the commercial stations by attracting the largest possible audience. In the end even public broadcasting institutions succumb to the effects of the ratings game. Mediocrity becomes the categorical imperative everywhere.

De Tocqueville revisited

The political dominance of mass taste raises other problems besides those of its effects on culture and everyday life. There is of course no question that individuals ought to be able to do whatever they please with their own lives and liberties within the bounds of law and morality. Yet it is questionable whether the tyranny of mass taste ought simply to be accepted as a fact of life in the sphere of politics, since politics helps determine the rules and life-chances that affect every single person, not to mention future generations. We can consider Alexis de Tocqueville as the true discoverer of the social rules that engender political mediacracy, i.e., the dominance of cultural and political mediocrity. Tocqueville, a political thinker whose origins were aristocratic but whose political leanings were democratic, was perhaps the first to diagnose the tendencies of mass democracy. While traveling through the world's first mass democracy, the still young United States of America, in 1831 and recording his impressions of it, Tocqueville was struck by the nearly irresistible pressure towards a leveling of public life. The least cultivated taste of the mass public, the taste of the average man, set the tone for public life generally. Competition for the favor of the mass public tends to grind down everything extraordinary, exceptional or just plain above average, since few want to risk displeasing the sovereign majority. When democracy seizes hold of culture, it makes anything that does not fit into majority tastes appear illegitimate.

What finally endangers democracy here is not its idea of political legitimacy, but instead the pressure toward equality that burdens public life by first ignoring and then extinguishing differences of education, knowledge, class, experience and taste. Yet these differences are the seed-bed which alone can nourish a civilized social existence, and a sense of personal independence and judgment. According to Tocqueville, "not only does democracy make every man forget his ancestors, but it hides his descendants and separates his contemporaries from him; it throws him back forever on himself alone and threatens in the end to confine him entirely within the solitude of his own heart."

Whereas the active, shared engagement of equal citizens in the associations of civil society fortifies their capacity for judgment and resistance against the centralism of egalitarian mediocrity, the equality of isolation imposes its rule over their thinking, culture, and lives. Under the somewhat misleading surface of Tocqueville's terminology lies the assessment that it is not democracy as practiced in its authentic form, i.e., as public deliberation oriented to consensus, but rather a combination of egalitarian isolation and majority tyranny that leads to the hegemony of mediocrity over the life and thought of an entire society.[11]

Thus, in light of Tocqueville's observations, there are really two mechanisms operating in tandem that lead to the prevailing mediocrity in culture and politics. First, there is the isolation of individuals, which predisposes them to bow to pressure and take their bearings in life from the average tastes and opinions of everyone around them. In this way, all members of society have a share in generating pressure to conform. The other mechanism involves the transference of the democratic principle of decision-making from politics into the social spheres of culture and lifestyle. In the former, democratic principles are at home, since they are held in check by rules stipulating basic rights; in the latter, they are suited to regulate the framework and foundations of culture but not to define its actual content. The egalitarian principle of majority legitimacy mutates from a rule governing political decision-making into a norm of cultural production that dominates all spheres of society equally. When that occurs, pressure is felt to impose the standards of mediocrity drawn from the low-average range across the board, since that will please the greatest number, and most people will support it immediately and at any time. It not only weaves its spell over political decisions, as it rightly should, but also on the public debates that precede those decisions. It finally pulls everything associated with democracy into its vortex.

Culture and politics

But we must distinguish two categorically different situations. On one hand, all individuals are entitled to decide how to provide for their own needs, and in particular to decide how closely they want to approach the lowest levels of the cultural and communicative spectrum in society, since these decisions primarily concern only the self.

On the other hand, when they want to turn the most abysmal cultural standards into authoritative guidelines for deciding what cultural and political fare should be most widely available and easily accessible, then that is obviously also of concern for the entire political community. One source of confusion between these situations is the tendency to treat the responsible citizen as though he or she were a private consumer.[12] When that happens, no one – neither the individual nor those with whom he or she comes into contact – can prevent the boundaries separating these quite distinct roles from blurring.

The left-wing critique of the culture industry fills volumes. What evoked it was disappointment at the fact that the masses had not benefitted from the highest cultural standards that society had made available up to that time. Even though democracy had been significantly expanded, social existence relieved of the crushing weight of poverty, coercion and hierarchy, and educational attainments notably increased, the cultural level of the masses was still discouragingly low. Apparently, inescapable competition to gain the largest possible clientele in the middle echelons of society, and even to reach its fringes, meant that henceforth norms would be established by the cultural strata with the most members. Patterns of behavior appropriate for consumers in the private sphere thus tended to spill over into the political public sphere, increasingly blurring the distinction between private and public. The plausible motto of the culture industry's planners was always: "the worm doesn't have to taste good to the fisherman, only to the fish." This is a rule that does not follow from any negligence or confusion of taste, but from the pressures of the media economy.

Television: commercial and public

In countries with public broadcasting networks, such as France, Italy, the United Kingdom and Germany, many intellectuals had long hoped that, on account of their relative insulation from the ratings game, they could offer high-quality programming in culture and politics. It was also hoped that they could raise quality standards for the media system as a whole and perhaps keep the dictatorship of banality at bay. But the appearance of private networks quickly showed that public broadcasting too was tightly yoked to the tyranny of the ratings system.[13] Just as water always finds its level in two connected vessels, so too the separate institutions of public and private broadcasting proved to be connected by unsuspected conduits that made ratings as constraining in the former as in the latter. There are two mechanisms that seem principally responsible for this state of affairs. One of these involves the ambitions of the programming chiefs inside the public broadcasting system itself. They want to catch up with their colleagues in the private networks in terms of public approval and mass influence, and thus win a game in which the rules and standards are inherently skewed in favor of the private broadcasters' way of operating. The other one is set in motion by segments of the political system. Certain conservative or technocratic politicians perpetually question the system of compulsory fees paid by the owners of television sets to support public broadcasting in some European countries. Their argument is always the same: why should citizens be forced to contribute fees for services that apparently do not fully meet their needs and which they would not choose on their own initiative?

In this way comparisons of audience shares and ratings between public and private broadcasts generate comparable pressures to maximize ratings throughout the entire system, regardless of the legal form of ownership and control. Under such circumstances the only remaining refuges for high-quality media productions, ones that do not necessarily need the legitimacy of high ratings, might include stations that specialize in late-night broadcasts or narrowly focused minority programming. Thus, in a mixed system, the logic of the mass media to a certain extent overshadows the independent ethos of public broadcasting, supposedly guaranteed by its distinctive legal status and pattern of ownership and control. The rules of successful mass communication become the basis for broadcasting success *per se*. Compared with the reach of mass communications, the influence of high-quality newspapers is marginal, and essentially limited to those cultural strata that already insulate themselves from standard broadcast fare, including eclectic media-users with a preference for intensive communication within their own circles. It is obvious that the prestige media do very little to inject an element of "culture" into mainstream fare. It is rather the reverse, with the former so far as possible adopting the lessons of the latter in order to survive in the media marketplace. In this sense Neil Postman is right to argue that television has become the cultural metaphor of the present age; it is a model of almost magical attractiveness, showing how other media can succeed.

The worm and the fish

As far as political communications are concerned, a bi-level pattern has emerged in the wake of the triumph of media rules, in both cases strengthening the hand of mediacracy. At the media level the trend is for politics to be presented in ever cruder, more trivialized and personalized ways in line with the rules governing the production of entertainment shows. The criterion governing media decisions about what to report and how to report it is, as always, to attract the most attention. The worm finally dangled in front of the fish has few discernible similarities left to anything that would have been palatable to the fisherman. But it is within the political process itself, the second level, that we encounter the truly significant chain of causation. The political actors themselves submit to the stage-management pressures of the media system. Politics ends up succumbing to the very same rules of staging and attention-maximizing that the media do, though not without a struggle for its soul. So it too evolves into a component of mediacracy. There are, as we have noted, certain features that make the political process and especially democratic politics what it is: more or less rational debate about well-articulated alternatives; the creation of programs and their controlled implementation; leisurely processes that transform interests and demands into achievable projects; an aspiration toward enlightenment through the clarification of particular interests via argument and counter-argument in the public space. All of these features are becoming unrecognizable or simply vanishing from the public's radar screen. Even the leading lights of the parties, succumbing to a stage-management pressure they never sought, must now direct and produce their own proposals and cast themselves as actors on a provincial stage, trying to win over the many unpersuaded voters in the audience.

Parasitic publicity

Measured against its voracious appetite for publicity, the capacity of the political system to produce newsworthy material still remains limited in spite of its increasing deployment of resources, ideas and stage-management skills. The solution to this news gap has been an almost boundless proliferation of strategies to wangle "parasitic" publicity. Assuming they have the necessary skills of self-presentation, politicians exhibit few inhibitions – and a great deal of imagination and creativity – in finding opportunities to turn up with people and in places that have already attracted media attention, even if they are not always welcome. Putting in a brief appearance on some of the public's favorite shows, and crowding the limelight wherever show-business celebrities turn up, have become familiar tricks of the trade. One example that could be cited is the Philippine hostage crisis of 2000. During the spring of that year a number of tourists were kidnaped by Philippine rebels from a nearby Indonesian resort and held on the island of Jolo, among them several German citizens. News coverage of this event in Germany, which dragged on until late summer, was very thorough in all its phases and in every venue. It became almost a textbook case displaying the entire palette of techniques whereby politicians could get parasitic publicity.

Category 1: journalists as co-actors   Journalists from several European countries sometimes crossed the line from being media observers to becoming direct participants in the hostage situation, for example, by carrying messages or going into the hostages' camp on their own initiative. A few even ended up being taken hostage themselves, and subsequently exploited their involvement in the kidnaping to add luster to their reports about the case and their own plight.

Category 2: politicians as unbidden ersatz heroes   The chief negotiator of the Philippine government, Aventejado, lost no opportunity to strike the appropriate statesman's poses in the course of his official communiqués, which attracted much media attention in the slower phases of the abduction. But beyond that he displayed a touching lack of inhibition in using the temporary disorientation of newly freed hostages to assume the pose of their savior, and thus give the media the images they sought. The fate of the hostages became so much raw material for the media, to be exploited for its stage-management value, without much heed being paid to their own interests and dignity.

Category 3: extorted publicity   The role of Libya and its revolutionary leader, Ghaddafi, in ransoming the hostages remains unclear. But his intervention became a major media event when he insisted, as a condition for their release, that the captives should make their first public appearance in the capital of his country, despite their months of suffering and the circuitous route they would have to take, and even before they were really free. At bottom, this coerced media event was nothing but the final act in the hostage drama itself.

Category 4: stealth publicity   In almost all phases of the freed hostages' journey back from the scene of their confinement to their home towns, political actors were continually thronging around them, getting as close as they possibly could, because these people were the focus of public interest. Usually the politicians' pretext was that they claimed a sort of functional or regional sovereignty over the staging-rights of the hostages' return. Everywhere in the Philippines the German ambassador took center stage. When they finally disembarked from the airplane, various ministers were waiting for them, claiming that their political responsibilities gave them a right to be there. When the freed hostages arrived at Hanover airport, an official reception awaited them hosted by several state ministers and the governor of the state of Lower Saxony; thereafter, they had to endure yet another reception in their home town, headed by the mayor and local dignitaries.

Category 5: the staged life-soap   Step by step, the media broadened their reports of the abduction and the abducted individuals, transforming it all into a "to-be-continued" story with no foreseeable end, even after the hostages had been freed and gone home. Daily they bestowed on their audiences pictures of the lives of the liberated individuals, their first-person impressions, tidbits of news from their locality, all designed to exploit publicity about the case as long as they possibly could. There were questions for the ex-hostages behind their houses and on their way to work, questions for their colleagues at work, for the neighbors; it went on until the last embers of attention had been extinguished. The media had engaged in a self-parasitic game of publicity maximization.

Parasitic publicity can occasionally bring priceless exposure for political actors. The ceremonies surrounding the one-hundredth birthday of the "Queen Mum" in Great Britain were a poignant reminder of that week after week. The royal family's chief representative, Prince Charles, especially profited from the carefully and pompously staged events, more indeed than he ever would have from media events focused directly on him. The media advisers of the royal family came to recognize the advantages for Prince Charles of these emotionally charged events, even though they were of course staged to celebrate a milestone in the life of the one truly beloved figure left in the royal family. The death of the media's darling, Princess Diana, had dealt a severe blow to Charles' public esteem, and the Queen Mother's birthday celebrations could be used to provide him with a media transfusion. So the staging of the jubilee was extended over many weeks in endless variations, and the nearly unlimited affection of the public for the centenarian was played out in a plethora of set showpieces. Journalists covering the ceremonies framed the many photogenic events with the oft-repeated declaration that the Prince was now the Queen Mother's favorite descendant, and their claims seemed borne out by the way he always turned up at her side at every public appearance, almost like her Siamese twin. The jubilee directors had managed to set up nearly every photo opportunity so that both the lovable royal grandmother's charming smile and the – by now more likable – Prince would appear in the same picture: parasitic publicity at the height of its powers.

It is not the equality of rights of all individuals, and certainly not their equal right to participate in the political association, but rather equality in isolation that ultimately makes everyone susceptible to the lowest common denominator of opinions, knowledge, norms, and judgment. This leveling tendency binds people together in an external, superficial way. They have opinions in common upon which they can agree, but do not have a common life with shared values. Their agreement however does create a public pressure to conform, which offers a substitute for the secure sense of orientation and identity that individuals can no longer find in their atomized isolation.

Pre-production and co-production

The Agora and the mass media

The media-dominated public sphere differs in principle from the model of the Agora, where citizens meet to deliberate on and decide about public affairs.[14] It is true that even ancient assembly democracy in its halcyon days never quite lived up to the ideal of argumentative action oriented to reaching consensus. The art of rhetoric as applied to public speech-making injected a stilted, artificial tone into its debates. Still, the fact that other members of the assembly were there to offer counter-arguments meant that publicly presented claims could always be submitted to critical examination and political convictions could be rationally scrutinized.

In contrast to the marketplace of ancient assembly democracy, the media-dominated public sphere functions in principle as a very exclusive stage to which access is strictly limited. As a rule the traditional theater stage was open to a wide variety of different kinds of plays, though accessibility differed from one era to the next. But the mass-media stage, particularly that of television, is subject to a complex and highly selective set of conditions for pre-producing or pre-staging events, which limits access and cannot easily be circumvented. The directors who control access to this stage exercise the strictest discipline in ensuring that the pre-production rules are followed, because they know their own success and even their survival hangs in the balance. They apply the same rigid controls to their own productions as they do when ordering or approving what other media personnel have created.

The rules for pre-productions in all of the mass media are derived from the logic of selection and presentation discussed earlier, which affect decisions about who and what gets on stage and may remain there for more than a fleeting instant. Television is the trend-setting medium, the one that largely sets the tone for the others, and to which political actors pay especially close attention in calculating their own media strategies. It has its own additional rules, both because it is not bound to a specific location, and because it relies so heavily on images. Pre-production determines the degree to which events in the world outside the media have to be reconstructed or reinterpreted in order to qualify for the media stage. It also influences the way actors outside the media prepare their own presentations to make them acceptable to the guardians of the media stage.

Because of its technical advantages, television can reach the widest possible audience with the most up-to-date, topical features, and in fact must do so for economic reasons. Accordingly, its pre-production rules bow to certain strict dictates: coverage should be as "pictorial" as possible, and everything should be presented so as to keep the audience on the edge of its chairs. Television owes its air of authenticity and directness, its skill at involving the viewers, to this pictorial quality, which makes features always seem convincing, at least initially. The tightened regimen of entertainment and non-stop excitement results from the tyranny of the remote control. Technology now makes it possible to ascertain via the remote exactly what the ratings of any show are at a given moment, which of course has enormous repercussions for the advertising revenues of commercial broadcast stations. But even public broadcasting is not spared, since

ratings give its productions standing and legitimacy before the political bodies that ultimately decide its funding level by setting the fees
described earlier.

Communication environments

The rules of pre-production establish the conditions under which the
media operate, and by extension also the communicative environment
created by it. Indeed, they actually constitute the media's *modus
operandi* and, almost unnoticed, define the essential content of what
is being communicated, without the recipients ever becoming aware
of their effects.[15] This silent dissimulation, the media's ability to divert
attention away from itself, is exactly what is required for it to function as a communications medium. On account of this automatic
dissimulation, we confront at the end of all the procedures, selection,
preparation, and stage-management an illusion, but one that appears
quite natural: we seem to be getting a direct view of reality as it is,
as if television were just an empty stage, where the actors and directors decided anew each time what we are going to see. Viewers experience the illusion of looking out through a window onto spatially
distant realities. This media *trompe l'œil* is the unique prize that com-
pensates them for their high costs and investments in technology on
the production side. In respect to the relationship between political
events and media construction, pre-production makes itself felt in the
tyranny of the numerous stage-management rules that must be mastered by politicians and their staffs of media consultants, as well as
by those who control access to the media stage. The pressure to stage-
manage seems to all the participants, both the creators of programming and the political actors, as though it were an impersonal force,
when in fact it emanates from the media themselves.

The rules of pre-production are hurdles political actors have to
overcome to gain access to the media stage. But there is no guarantee that access will be on terms they would prefer, or that their projects will be aired in the manner that they had intended. In the final
analysis it is always the creators of media products who act as gate-
keepers in regulating the manner and extent of access. The finished
product supplied by the media is thus nearly always a co-production,
in which political actors offer their creations and media actors transform them, in fact sometimes even utterly ruin them. So media figures
too are still fulfilling the staging conditions of their medium when
they first dissect and then reconstruct the productions they have

obtained from the political sphere. Even though political actors may have internalized thoroughly the criteria of pre-production, the media may still prefer to follow their own interpretation of these rules and repackage the production according to a different set of interests. Or, for that matter, they may decide to give the public a surprise look behind the scenes, where the craft of production is practiced, to reveal how the stage-managing of politics really works. The economics and strategies of the media prevent this sort of thing from occurring very often, but in principle it always remains possible. Such adversarial forms of synthesis between the productions offered by politics and the media's own directorial discretion are much more costly and therefore less financially attractive than would be the case if the media simply aired whatever the politicians gave them. Moreover, they can lead to conflicts with the affected politicians and are therefore strategically unattractive, since they might make it more difficult in the future to gain access to information from this source. Thus, co-productions by the media and the world of politics can – but do not have to – be symbiotic. The pressure to stage-manage, generated by the trend toward pre-production for the media stage, has tended to make political communication one of the chief concerns of the political system itself in media democracy. Indeed the success and legitimacy of political action hinges on how well political communication is handled.

Of course, the sovereign power to manage the media stage still remains in the hands of media actors, at least in principle. However perfectly done a political production may have been in terms of the media's rules, there is still no guarantee that it will be aired by the media just as it is, without changes. When agents outside the media try to anticipate and adjust to the way the media will likely want to stage something, they may increase the chances that the media will leave their production unaltered. But in the end it is the media actors themselves who decide on the whether, the how, and the when of access. Of course, depending on the type of media they work for, they too are under a threefold set of pressures that varies in degree: competition from other media; the economy of production costs; and the need to secure continuing access to as many primary sources of information as possible. For these reasons pre-production constraints regularly give rise to strategies of symbiotic co-production, i.e., varying forms of collaboration between the productions served up by the political world, and whatever final stage-managing the media authors choose to perform on these.

Politics by trial balloon

The eminent Zurich-based communications scientist, Otfried Jarren, has proposed a new interpretation of the mutual interactions between the media and politics.[16] It is already clear that policies conceived outside of the media have to be stage-managed. But Jarren suggests that the interplay between the media and policy-makers begins earlier, when the main political actors are at the policy-planning stage. Thus, the policy dimension, once considered exogenous to the media, now appears as an endogenous element. His description captures an important strand in the logic of a politics colonized by the media. Yet when it is understood as a model depicting the whole gamut of relationships between the two spheres, it can also conceal decisively important features therein. In principle there is still an ontological difference between actions taken to implement political decisions and the way those actions are represented in the media. Indeed, we neglect that difference at our peril. But despite these caveats the model does highlight a significant new tendency of political action in media democracy.

The handling of major reform proposals by the red-green government in the German Federal Republic since it took office in September, 1998 offers an example of this tendency, since its actions can be understood only as a series of media-oriented trial runs orchestrated by top-echelon political actors. The government, committed to implementing long-standing positions that had been taken by party resolutions or in the negotiations between coalition partners, unveiled a series of reform projects that, in effect, came half-finished right out of its workshop. These were introduced as designs or intentions, not as full-fledged proposals. That way, if media reaction seemed unfavorable, they could be withdrawn, revised and presented again in a new form, but without the leadership ever consulting party members to insure themselves of the latter's continuing support. This practice of sending up media trial balloons, and, if these were shot down, revising the plan and sending up a new trial balloon continued until one of two things happened. Either the proposals passed the media test, or else the politicians came to the conclusion that they had a better chance of passing an alternative plan later on, and gave up for the time being. In all these instances the logic of events unfolded as a kind of bargaining between the original programmatic intentions of the top political actors and the media's response to these, frequently in a multi-stage process, and occasionally in a very short time. When reform plans were announced concerning the social insurance aspects of short-term, occasional employment, the ping-pong game between political trial run and media response was accelerated to a breathtaking speed. Within a few short weeks great and consequential reform proposals were "improved" or exchanged for other ones.

In this bargaining process the media claim to be rendering a public verdict, which might very well go against the politicians in the next election. But in truth they are really not so much reflecting public judgments as shaping them. To review one highly informative example of this distinction, the media recently responded with almost unanimous approval to the German government's package of pension and tax reforms. Yet surveys revealed that the public did not really understand the proposals. Pensioners and lower-income citizens, drawing on their own experiences, sensed that they would not be the winners in this round of reform, one that incidentally would touch their vital interests. A borderline case such as this creates a dilemma for government officials. They know from experience and professional acumen that the public sphere controlled by the media on the whole both shapes and reflects majority opinion as well as the voters' electoral verdict. But they also realize that such a rule cannot be relied upon in individual situations. Only in rare and exceptional cases would it be advisable for a top political actor dependent on majority support to defy current media responses and hope that future electoral majorities will rally behind his program. In a media democracy these rare instances must be calculated carefully in advance because of the risks involved. In this sense most crucial political proposals take shape as bargaining processes carried on under the klieg lights of media reactions. Their tendency is to shift from being exogenous to endogenous events within the media. Nevertheless, the intensification of this tendency does not mean that the exogenous and endogenous dimensions of action are destined to merge. The policy program that is implemented at the end of the negotiating process between media and politics has an independent reality not exhausted by its depiction in the media or by whatever the politicians in charge make of it in their media events. The law that is finally passed, together with all its intended and unintended consequences, may be something more than and quite different from what was anticipated and how it is depicted in the media. Neither the negotiations between the media and politicians in the glare of public attention, nor the political actors' efforts to put a favorable spin on it can ever quite obliterate the sheer unpredictability inherent in human action, or the gap between reality and its representation.

In the context of media democracy's underlying logic and the basic issues it raises, there are two salient points to be made. First, of course, is the one just mentioned: that the reality of political action and its consequences remains ontologically distinct from the way it is represented. More interesting, though, are the implications of this distinction for democratic politics. Media constructions can never simply mirror, or even unambiguously reconstruct, either the internal richness and relative importance of details or the complex ramifications of political action. But there is a second reason why the bargaining process between the media and politics can never lead to a convergence of these subsystems. The media spotlight can never illuminate more than a small slice of the plenitude of policy projects that are being planned or readied for implementation in the political-administrative system at any given time. They may often manage to touch some of the most important ones, but never all of them or all aspects of the ones they do highlight. Thus, although politics by trial balloon may become a common strategy in media democracy, it will not result in the merger of the political and media systems. In the transitional phase between party and media democracy in Europe current at the start of the twenty-first century, with party organizations still vital enough that, if they put their minds to it, they could turn the bargaining process between politics and media to their own advantage, they could thus reconfigure the parallelogram of forces resulting from it.

The anaesthesia effect

Throughout the Monica Lewinsky scandal and subsequent impeachment, former President Clinton managed to cling to office despite an unparalleled media campaign against him, and the apparently well-substantiated charge that he had made false statements in a court of law. In the last analysis his near immunity to the vendetta against him rested on what we might call the anaesthesia effect. Amid the flood of details the public gradually lost its ability to distinguish between real events that demanded a moral judgment, and media fabrications staged and exaggerated for effect. The media had "cried wolf" one too many times, and the public had become cynical. In this sense the media unintentionally played into the politicians' hands. In a similar case, the German CDU campaign finance scandal that began in December of 1999 and dragged on through the entire next year demonstrated another side of the anaesthesia effect that a public sphere dominated by the mass media can engender. The point is not simply that the media-dominated public sphere's obsession with the present and its rules of dramatic staging dull our sensibilities to the point where we need ever higher doses of media fare to achieve the same stimulation as before. Rather, the anaesthesia effect arises as a direct, ineluctable result of the media's rules of production. In an unfolding story the only elements that count as newsworthy are unexpected twists and quantitative advances in well-established plot elements. Since a surprising twist in a familiar storyline seems almost as newsworthy as a completely new revelation, two tendencies emerge from this pattern of reportage. It may cut a shallow meandering channel through the informational environment of the initial event, or encourage reporters to bore ever more diligently into deeper strata. Sometimes the outcome is a disjunction between the real events and their media depiction, to the point that the average reader or viewer has scarcely any chance of evaluating the importance and magnitude of what is happening in the world beyond the media. In the Clinton case, reporter Sam Donaldson stood before the White House after the Lewinsky scandal broke and intoned that the end of his pre-sidency was probably only hours away. Viewers had no way of knowing whether Clinton really intended to resign, or whether the media was pushing him toward the exit by making self-fulfilling prophecies. In such cases the public understandably feels less certain of its ability to scrutinize events intelligently and accurately; its powers of judgment are seriously compromised.

Consequently, neither the active nor the passive part of the media audience can ever quite escape the impression that a great deal of the hue and cry and the frenetic pace that initially seem inherent in reported events are in many cases actually supplied by the media themselves. Two of the accused in the CDU campaign finance scandal, former Chancellor Helmut Kohl and the Governor of Hesse, Roland Koch, adopted distinct strategies to ward off the bad publicity of continuing media revelations. Yet both counted on the effect just described. Kohl again followed his tried-and-tested recipe of refusing to comment on the main points of the accusations and leaving reporters with nothing to cover. He evidently hoped – not without good reason – that the public and eventually even the most dogged media actors would finally lose interest. By contrast, Roland Koch tried more of an interventionist strategy. Certain that except for the reporters on his case nobody would ever be able to keep straight all the details of the chain of events, the facts, and the data, he declared that every new revelation was actually an old one, which had already been presented in the "media circus." He abjured all putative public responsibility for the affair, repeating that it was nothing but the usual media game. Koch's attempt to dismiss what had happened as a media event, as though the media had once again created an unfounded story, may not always achieve success. Nevertheless, his strategy enabled him to remain in office well into the twenty-first century in spite of the well-documented accusations that, in the traditional political culture of the Federal Republic, would have led to any other politician's resignation.

The public now realizes that the media will not hesitate to offer excessive doses of attention-getting effects. The politicians know that the public is aware of this tendency, and they factor the effect into their communications strategy as a way of evading media scrutiny. In the long run, the anaesthesia phenomenon undermines democratic accountability by making citizens lose confidence in their ability to distinguish media frenzy from politicians' genuine deficiencies.

Summary

Despite strong tendencies toward the colonization of politics by the rules of the media system, there is no question that the logic of political processes continues to define political competition, even as the influence of media logic keeps spreading. Actors pursue interests, even when the media dominate the circumstances under which they act. They wield various power resources, among which the availability of the mass media plays a new and crucial role. And they use social, economic, and media power to shape events. Although the inherent logic of political action may indeed be modified, supplemented, or accentuated in new ways in the course of a political process now thoroughly dominated by the logic of the media, the latter will never entirely displace or absorb political logic.

Under the influence of its given cultural environment and the basic rules of media logic journalism itself becomes more and more a part of the popular culture of its time. This tendency to mix different types of discourses under the influence of their most successful popular forms prevails in all parts of the media system. The dominance of the aesthetics of popular culture may, however, serve either professional journalistic ends or exclusively entertainment interests, or a variety of types of mixtures of both of them. Consequently, in the course of the colonization of the political system by the rules of media discourses, a substantial part of politics tends to follow the same trend. To that degree politics itself becomes politainment, a form of popular culture.

In contrast to the marketplace of ancient assembly democracy, the media-dominated public sphere functions in principle as a very exclusive stage, access to which is strictly limited. The mass-media stage, particularly that of television, is subject to a complex and highly selective set of conditions for pre-producing or pre-staging events, which limits access and cannot easily be circumvented. The rules for pre-productions in all of the mass media are derived from the logic of selection and presentation discussed earlier, which affect decisions about who and what gets on stage and may remain there for more than a fleeting instant. It also influences the way actors outside the media prepare their own presentations to make them acceptable to the guardians of the media stage.

Under the pressure of media pre-production policy programs tend to be introduced as trial balloons, not as full-fledged proposals. That way, if media reaction seems unfavorable, they can be withdrawn, revised and presented again in a new form. In all these instances the logic of events unfolds as a kind of bargaining between the original programmatic intentions of the top political actors and the media's response to these, frequently in a multi-stage process, and occasionally in a very short time. Consequently, the process of political deliberation in the public sphere and those aspects of the political logic and system that represent the long time-frame of the political process tend to become increasingly marginalized.

5

The Transformation of Representative Democracy

The marginalization of representative democracy

Most recent studies in the future of mediated politics focus on the changes of the public sphere or on the relations between the public sphere and the polity sphere.[1] In this section I would like to carry the discussion one step further and investigate the ongoing transformation in the political structures and processes proper, particularly with respect to parties, parliaments and the intermediary sector.

The decline of political parties

Throughout the 1990s political parties as mass organizations lost much of their significance in the larger European countries like Italy, Germany and Great Britain. Their role as elements in political power struggles waned, and they no longer had as much influence over societal discourses as they once did. In spite of some hastily initiated reforms, their membership base also dwindled significantly. Until the start of the twenty-first century the parties had three central functions in the political process. These involved both the normative standards of parliamentary democracy and the parties' practical responsibilities too, since they still had so much day-to-day influence on politics and the shaping of public opinion. First, they collated the political interests articulated by a wide array of associations, interest groups, citizens' lobbies and organizations into a few proposals that stood a chance of achieving society-wide legitimacy. Second, they transmitted those socially articulated interests to the political system, especially at the level of parliament and government. Third, they had always recruited candidates and enabled them to run for office, whence, once in positions of power, these officials could insure the implementation of the party's platform. By virtue of this threefold bridging function, the parties succeeded in moving parliamentary democracy beyond the traditional liberal pattern in which individuals represented the popular will but lacked any specific, binding mandate. In Germany this approach has always been evident in Article 38 of the Basic Law.

As the Constitutional Court Justice Gerhard Leibholz noted, the parties implicitly converted democracy into a kind of issue plebiscite, since by voting for a party the voters are also issuing a programmatic mandate. By contrast, media democracy, as exemplified more and more unmistakably in US presidential elections, strongly predisposes voters to give their consent to the person of the candidate as a "media artist" rather than to the programs he or she has been advocating. It must be conceded, however, that the pattern of American elections was set long before the rise of modern media democracy, and has a great deal to do with the decentralized, fragmented electoral system of the country. Mediacracy would be weaker and parties stronger in the United States if electoral laws were revised to favor straight-ticket party voting, and if parties had more control over the selection of their own candidates. In any case the transition in Germany's political system from party to media democracy involved a switch from issue plebiscites to personal plebiscites with far-reaching consequences for the role of political parties in the process of legitimation.

All along the line, the logic of media democracy has forced parties out to the fringes of events, even though they may still capture public attention through their activity in local politics and their residual power to set a tone and direction for the leadership.[2] Under the hammer of media logic, there is a tendency for the communications strategies of the party leadership to lose contact with the rank-and-file and lose patience with its snail-paced deliberations. This disjunction is largely due to the relentless media pressure for immediate reactions and to trial balloons sent up by the politicians: in short, the media's "presentism," which leaves no time for the leadership to consult the grass-roots party councils. In the United States, these trends have reached the point where political parties have even lost their old "kingmaker" function, once the guarantor of their unique role in the political process and their continuing control over the policies of elected officials. There, the system of primary elections has slowly shifted preeminence in the selection of candidates from the parties' inner councils to the media. To win a primary election, a candidate often needs to have appeal in the media, since that will translate into political support and victory at the polls. Electoral laws in most states require the party to remain neutral in the primaries *vis-à-vis* the candidates, which effectively removes them from the process and, by elimination, pushes the campaign almost entirely into media channels. The inherent dynamics of media democracy thus have a tendency to assign the parties only a "bit part" in the drama of the broader political process. As communities of democratic discourse and decision with impressive grass-roots memberships, parties may go on for a long time as though nothing had changed, upholding the old rules, processes, and rituals, and claiming the right to establish authoritatively the broad outlines of policy for their political representatives. Yet in terms of their *de facto* opportunities to affect policy, they are moving from the center to the margins of the political process in media democracy.

Media communication v. party logics

During the postwar era in the United States, the favorable image of a potential presidential candidate in the major media, especially television, has been the key criterion in securing his nomination. Even the parties looked on with fascination during the primaries, to see which of their candidates would be the media's darling, which left them with little to do but put their stamp of approval on whomever the media in effect had chosen. In no sense did American elections ever function in accordance with democratic theory, i.e., as a competition between alternative political programs hammered out by the parties after significant citizen participation. Instead, they were mainly horse-races that tested the media fitness of the candidates and their skill at embodying the broad moods of the public in the symbolism of their self-presentation. Looking comparatively at more recent developments, it is true that Tony Blair had prepared the ground for his assumption of the leadership of the Labour Party by reforming the party and defeating the ultra-left in 1995. But his amazingly strong opinion-survey results prior to the 1997 election and his subsequent convincing win gave him the overwhelming media backing he needed to marginalize the internal discourses, first of his party and then of its contingent in Parliament. By and large, he accomplished this by shutting down internal debates, manipulating them from above or simply ignoring them. Likewise in Germany, the skillfully staged race between potential SPD Chancellor candidates Gerhard Schröder and Oskar Lafontaine in the 1998 elections stirred up considerable media interest by a clever ploy.[3] It was made known by the party leadership that the candidate who did the best in state elections would eventually be chosen as the SPD's candidate. This announcement had the effect of short-circuiting intra-party debates, in which it is expected that internal communications will be kept confidential. In the end it was even suggested that the high-profile state contests were a superior form of democratic legitimation compared to intra-party controversy. These developments show that the marginalization of parties does not always imply that they lack significance. But their role shift from center stage to the periphery of the political process, an artefact of the media's internal laws, portends an uncertain future for traditional European party democracy.

In light of this logic, even political scientists like J. Raschke who are committed to grass-roots democracy have argued in favor of distancing the upper echelons of the party's communications structure from its political base. They claim that, without considerable independence from rank-and-file opinion, the leadership will not easily be able to implement the policies the party supports, because to succeed on the issues they need freedom to maneuver in the media arena. Given the short interval between political initiatives and media responses to them, and the equally short time-frame in which leaders must react, the party would be tying leaders' hands and condemning them to failure if it insisted that they wait for party decisions to authorize their every move. In the rapid-fire sequence of initiative and response, the party leadership allegedly needs to react as quickly as the media does. It is clearly not in the party's interest to hamper its leaders' ability to implement its program. So a contradiction arises between one political orientation that puts a premium on success in achieving political goals, and another that sees parties as discursive organizations and favors more political participation inside them.

The risk of launching a long-term "campaign to enlighten the public" against the tide of majority opinion, however transient, is usually too great for most upper-echelon political representatives to contemplate. Given the pressures of competition for the top leadership posts, they rarely have the luxury of undertaking a deliberate process in which the better arguments eventually would outweigh unfavorable initial impressions and lead to a new majority. The rare exceptions to their reluctance would be cases in which there were palpable indications that a strategy of popular enlightenment might succeed in the foreseeable future.

As we have already seen, the dominance of mass taste over the political sphere in media democracy, what we might call the mediocrity of mediacracy, arises from the isolation of individual selves in this kind of society.[4] But it is also linked to the hegemony of "media time" over the public sphere. Any public that is given sufficient time and freedom from constraints can ultimately reach a reasonably enlightened consensus about what is necessary, just, sustainable and responsible. But communications that transpire in the media's time-horizon tend instead to pin down and harden inchoate opinions and moods into immutable prejudices. These can then be cited, in a masterful bit of circular, self-reinforcing logic, as justification for protecting democracy from too much public participation. Finally the media add together opinions, an aggregate total against which it is useless to offer alternatives, go through the process of argument, or develop implications. The staccato beat of repetitive positions, even when these are in some ways open to learning processes and corrections, leaves no room for deliberation oriented to finding a consensus. Thus, both the tyranny of mass tastes and the rigidity of opinion in media democracy have a common root: the isolation of the individual from the contexts of public discussion and exchange of ideas.

The threatened intermediary sector

The demotion of intermediate actors to a secondary status within media democracy is a consequence of the tyranny of media time over political time. Without these actors it is no longer possible to articulate the interests of society and continually remind its members that they have a common life and shared concerns. The intermediary associations try to achieve consensus through deliberation; even when they fail, they raise the awareness level of society as a whole. This happens because, in mediating between state and society, they express the latter's diffuse expectations and experiences, converting them into demands for specific political measures. Thus, not only do they generate the raw material and essential energy of the political system, but they concurrently forge bonds of solidarity that promote social integration. Traditionally, political parties played a double role in this

process. On the one hand they sought to integrate particular interests into proposals that could gain society-wide support. On the other
hand, when they succeeded at the polls and assumed the reins of government, they sought to implement and take responsibility for their
programs. But under the prevailing conditions of media democracy,
above all the logic of its time-schedules, they are more and more
pushed out to the exurbs of politics. The political process that takes
place within society, which parties once embodied and enabled, thus
exchanges its erstwhile role as the primary channel of influence upon
the "finished product" of politics for the status of marginal player.
The leading political actors of course still pay attention to it, and
sometimes try to enlist it for their own advantage, but normally only
within the limits of the media game, which are becoming more restric-
tive all the time.

The time-poor and the time-rich

It has been argued that the changing time-dimensions of modern
society, especially its accelerated tempo, have marginalized parties
in yet another sense. The people who work in the top jobs of the contemporary knowledge- and service-based economy are under
constant time pressure from their professional responsibilities. They
cannot afford to invest their skills in the time-consuming, snail-paced
processes of political consultation and opinion formation typical of
political parties. So those who do attend party gatherings tend more
and more to be people with spare time: local government officials,
teachers, homemakers, retirees, drop-outs and adherents of a self-
consciously slower-paced lifestyle. Whether stemming from more
relaxed job demands or a conscious choice to cultivate a less frenetic
tempo, they have enough time for the extended, continuing participation in party affairs needed to attain influence and success there.
The very different temporal cultures and budgets of the time-rich and
time-poor result from their respective positions in the economy and
the divergent social cultures they encourage. According to the argument, the inherent selectivity exercised by time factors distorts the
demography of political party membership, rendering parties as mass
organizations far less representative of the wider society than they
once were. The point is that, on account of this trend, the strategic
centers of party leadership have no real choice but to marginalize the
rank-and-file, since they are forced to try to build majorities in the
entire society. If the leaders do not succeed in doing so, they will end

up as the captives of a minority consensus shaped by the "logic" of party loyalists with time on their hands; in the long run they will not be able to keep the party abreast of the changing values, perceptions of interest, and opinions that emerge from evolutionary social processes. Accordingly, the more that the strategic power centers in the parties loyally uphold the values of the rank-and-file, the less able they are to succeed in the business of building political majorities through professional, flexible tactics. Democratic mass parties, which are actually supposed to be the transmission belts between society and the system of political institutions, have instead become barriers between society and political power. Although this pessimistic assessment of the parties' dilemma exaggerates some things, it does capture a real social trend. However, it neglects to mention that individuals ultimately have a choice in whether or not they are "time-poor," and generally about how to spend their time.

The "mediazation" of politics is thus generating a conflict between different tempos to which politics itself may eventually succumb. Abbreviating the time interval normally demanded by the political process down to what the media's production schedule permits means abridging the entire process by deleting the procedural components that qualify it as democratic. Discursive exchanges between participating actors give way to a series of self-correcting media trial runs carried out by top-echelon office-holders and their media consultants. Germany's decision to abandon nuclear power would not have been possible or even accepted by broad strata of the population if its "fundamentalist" advocates had chosen to submit it to a referendum early in the debates on the issue.

The dictatorship of the present moment

The process of maturation that applies to political problem-solving includes both dimensions: majority coalition-building in society and a more precise definition of the strategies to be adopted to solve the problems efficaciously. But media time does not allow decisions to mature, as it is wedded to the immediate present, an almost Cartesian or geometric point in time having no extension. Media time insists that everything be absolutely current and up to date; even the return message by courier is too slow, since the information it contains would be obsolete even before it arrived. Media time is thus not a continuous process, like development or dialogue, but the ceaseless accumulation of unconnected "nows." The media's presentism, in other words, shows no patience or understanding for politics' slower pace and process character as it methodically considers programs for action and allows majority convictions to take shape. Instead it caters to the transitory opinions of the public, pins them down and in fact indirectly reinforces them by way of repetition and cultivation. Moreover, media presentism insists that politics immediately endorse the public's every ephemeral whim, which it has assiduously reflected, focused and recorded. Everywhere its influence reaches, then, media-oriented politics imposes a time-horizon that is incompatible with democracy's inherent tempo.

Modified temporal relationships play a consequential role for political parties in three distinct respects:

1   As organizations committed to discourse and interest-integration, parties are too slow-moving to keep up with the presentism typical of media communications.
2   They are exceptionally attractive to citizens whose occupational situation and lifestyle leaves them enough time, or who simply make time, for political consultations.
3   As the preeminent organizations in the system of intermediary bodies, they are losing a good portion of their effectiveness at integrating diverse interests and opinions, because the intermediary sector as a whole has been forced to the sidelines of the political process.

The criteria of selectivity in the temporal structures of media democracy diminish the parties' role, without completely devaluing it. However, the media's dominance over political communication devalues much of the very process by which political matters are communicated or transmitted throughout the system. To be sure, parties can always adapt to the changed temporal structures, to win back lost influence in new ways. In addition to the American model, we can now begin to discern the outlines of a European model of party behavior. Here the parties reorganize their communicative patterns to gain influence within civil society, thus preventing their exclusion from the centers of decision-making. But the parties' weaknesses will continue to surface whenever the media's communications dynamics require quick reactions to current events, and wherever the day-to-day exigencies of the national political scene demand practical implementation of political principles in the direct media spotlight. Parties are by nature unsuited to this sort of thing, and their deficiencies in both cases are massive and probably beyond remedy. At their current stage of development parties show no signs of having devised any reforms that could restore their old preeminence in either domain. Their strengths, which neither the practices of elite party communicators nor media communications processes can ever supplant, will become especially conspicuous whenever long-term political projects are at issue, in which continuity of personnel and accountability matter a great deal. In such cases what count most are the political principles and basic, trend-setting decisions taken at the highest levels of politics, as well as the communication and day-to-day practical politics occurring at the grass-roots level, in civil society and in local government.

Curran, Smith and Wingate conclude that the most important outcomes of the mass media are not to be sought in their repercussions for the political system, but rather in their pacifying effects on the public ("conservative policing of the consensus").[5] I would like to defend the contrary argument that the most far-reaching consequences of the mass media are precisely the changes they have wrought in the political process. The latter are far more profound than those authors suppose, since they transform the political process itself. By marginalizing parties and the intermediary system, the media diminish the opportunities that civil society might have to exert influence on political inputs. So even if a more critical political consciousness should emerge in a citizen body, its members' opportunities for influencing politics would already have been limited in advance.

Who holds power in media democracy?

Events and internal power arrangements at the US presidential nominating conventions in 2000 revealed, almost as though under a magnifying glass, the structures and processes that define the *ideal type of media democracy*. What matters in these conventions are not only the highly public roles and political prominence of the actors who formulate and implement policy, but also the distinctive contributions of the shadowy figures who hone the politicians' images. Of course, the conventions are but a small, highly concentrated and rather atypical slice of the US political process. Yet for that reason they shed

light on an important component of its political logic, which
tinguished by the interplay of seven elements.

1   The entire nominating convention, supposedly held s
party delegates can select a presidential candidate and approve an
electoral platform, is actually planned from the very beginning as a
media event. The party's strategic elite stage-manage it as such, at
least the visible, media-accessible aspects of it. The elements of discourse, pluralism, issue-oriented debate and genuine decision-making
by the party delegates that once characterized the "classic" conventions of democratic mass parties no longer play much of a role. The
last remnants of open decision-making and discursive interaction
among the assembled delegates – i.e., of politics inside the parties –
have been purged. Now the goal is to flawlessly portray the party as
a mere ambience reflecting the charismatic personality of the newly
anointed candidate, all in strict conformity to media rules of presentation. The event is staged almost as though the delegates were await-
ing redemption on Judgment Day, with the presidential candidate
playing the redeemer's role. As a rule he no longer even takes part in
the proceedings of the entire convention. Instead, he schedules his
appearance as the climactic event of the final day, when he arrives to
share his redeeming thoughts with the assembled faithful in his convention address, the scintillating culmination of the whole affair. The
convention itself is made to seem little more than a prelude, an
opening act warming up the crowd for the appearance of the candidate himself, who outshines everyone and everything, but whose
address usually pays no attention to what the delegates have been
saying and doing for the past few days.

2   Behind the scenes, and well away from the glare of publicity,
small working groups hammer out the party's platform for the
coming election. It is officially intended to set the basic agenda of
the next president's policies, although most candidates respond to
situations as they arise and refer to the platform only when con-
venient. Since the convention delegates do not know exactly what
the candidate will say in his address as they put together the party
platform, and since he has a free hand in writing his speech and
laying out his program, it appears that neither document is binding
on the other. In some vague way, the party's policy proposals
contribute to the ambience surrounding the leading figure in the
drama, but they are never understood as IOUs that the successful
candidate must either honor once in office or risk losing legitimacy.

We might call this model of political message-sending "unregulated ambiguity." While the policy proposals emanating from the party are ultimately non-binding, they are still fairly concrete, so the more actively engaged citizens will tend to read them as commitments. By contrast, the candidate's positions are more calculated to win the support of the passive, communicatively disengaged citizens. Although they do not pin him down to anything very specific, they can serve still as the bona fides of his inner vocation for office, and give him an excuse to put some distance between himself and the party's official positions.

3   The presidential candidate himself, who so far has not taken any overt part in the proceedings or their communications, now begins a carefully orchestrated journey to the convention site, during which he will make several planned stops to check in with the assembled delegates and journalists via live TV broadcasts, in anticipation of his painstakingly stage-managed arrival. Toward the end of the convention he descends upon the throng in a grand finale as though he were a higher-order being. The ritual makes clear that he does not owe his position as the party's favorite to the delegates, but to the *higher powers of public relations* that have chosen and consecrated him. He communicates this message to the delegates in a twofold sense. He proclaims his program to them in a way designed to assure its – and their – superiority in the media game. And he allows them to bask for a few hours in his media charisma.

In his closing address, a kind of secular revelation, he lays down the gospel which the delegates have had absolutely no part in formulating and which they will never have a chance to debate once it has been proclaimed. The higher media message the candidate delivers is entirely his affair. Everybody knows that his team of spin-doctors have carefully designed, prepped, and staged it for the benefit of the media anyway. The last remnants of a classic party convention proceeding, in which the candidate himself actually played an active role in the deliberations and eventually stumped for the program that emerged from the discourse of the assembled delegates, by now have been entirely eradicated.

4   Just as important as what the candidate says in his speech are the *messages woven into the entertainment* segments of the broadcast. Presented as images, they are meant to have an effect independent of the candidate's words; in fact, in the case of the 2000 Republican Convention, they conveyed nearly the opposite messages from the ones found in the candidate's and party's declarations of

principle. An ethnically diverse dance troupe appeared on stage, for example, representing many of the groups from whom the party and its candidate wanted to win electoral support. The way it was done, and the kind of emphasis put on it, were meant to suggest that the party cared deeply about cultivating racial harmony and promoting the ethnic groups' most important concerns. The vague proposals and well-known political profile of the candidate hardly amounted to a program of action that would promise many advantages to American ethnic minorities. Yet they were presented as the darlings of the Republican Party in the theatrically staged segments of the convention's "show," which in turn served as a centerpiece of the media broadcasts from the convention. Clearly, the ethnic groups did not get the message, since African Americans voted for Gore by a ratio of nearly 9 to 1, and Hispanics by a 2 to 1 margin.

5   The choreography of the entire event follows the *cultural pattern of carnival* or *mardi gras*. There are costumes, dancing, musical rhythms, balloons floating skyward, waving placards, pictures, and emblems. And a mood of boisterous jubilation, even ecstasy seems to sweep over the visual spaces and events. It is a festive, light-hearted crowd full of cheer and great expectations, too good-natured to want to have petty debates, and too sure of victory to need them anyway. These are people, in short, who are convinced of the rightness of their cause, at peace with themselves. They have no wish to be caught up in pathetic little debates; instead they want to infect everyone else with their overflowing enthusiasm.

6   Meetings are frequently held on the fringes of the main events to make binding political decisions, yet the media often learn little about them, and they are kept carefully sealed off from the more public stages. In *adjacent rooms*, out of reach of the delegates and cameras, the candidate's confidantes accept donations from the big corporations and interest groups and promise to listen to their "concerns." Although neither the donors nor the recipients of the money presume that a direct, binding, cash-for-favors deal has been consummated, everyone understands that money is changing hands for a reason. Both sides try to calculate the political value of what is given, and how it might be compensated; that is the unspoken premise of the whole procedure. In exchange for helping political actors acquire power, the donors ensure that their interests will be looked after. Much of what will really be done once the campaign's spell is broken gets decided here, in the course of these small transactions behind the scenes of the media stage. They are not actually a

formal part of the nominating process. It merely provides a con-
venient venue for them to be negotiated.

7   At no time do the *participants* ever have a chance to debate
the crucial aspects of the conventions they are attending: how the
whole meeting is to unfold, what the candidate will say in his address
or how he presents himself in public. Instead the delegates themselves
are simply stage-management props, objects of an event that has been
concocted and implemented by professional media consultants under
the aegis and control of the candidate. A considerable portion of the
big money accepted in the back rooms ends up in their pockets as
commissions for their services.

The elements of this event and its contextual patterns highlight in
a nearly ideal-typical way crucial aspects of the logic of the political
process in media democracy. They reveal a great deal about the connections between the visible and recondite aspects of the process, the
strategic planning and collaboration involved in it, the roles of delegates and party rank-and-file, the media, and the stars, and compress
all these insights into just a few eventful days. Politics in a nutshell.
The open secret of media democracy, its condition *sine qua non*, is
that it achieves its intended effect even though the end-product has
been so obviously stage-managed, and the intentions behind it are so
clear to everyone.

Prospects for party democracy

Whether the marginalization of political parties in Europe will ever
reach the point it has in the United States since World War II remains
an open question. There are three quite distinct positions that have
emerged in European mass parties, both at the level of reform debates
and among the leadership cadres as they weigh their options for internal party reform.

The first model simply advocates a defense of the old way of doing
things. Its adherents may be convinced that the traditional party
model still has life in it, or they may be fighting tooth-and-nail to
defend hard-won and zealously guarded positions of power within
mid-level party organizations. But in any case they resist calls for
serious reform.

The successful campaign and business manager of one of Europe's
largest mass parties, Germany's CDU, embodies the second model.
He argued for almost twenty years that mass parties of the classical

European type have become outmoded under the impact of modern communications techniques. Professional media consultants prepare communications, while the political leadership takes responsibility for them. But only the parties' much greater access to financial resources today can set the machinery of modern political communications in motion. Thus, it is the talents of the strategic communications consultants and the politicians' ability to raise funds to carry out their designs that will ultimately bestow success on parties in the age of media democracy. Anything beyond that should be considered at best a customer-relations matter, concerning citizens with specific problems, and should be handled by the party's elected representatives. In other words, democracy in the media age means fund-raising for sophisticated communications plus a little constituent service. In this model parties again become "machines" (Max Weber), since they are ultimately geared only to pass on centrally planned communicative strategies from the top to the bottom of the chain of command. If one accepts this model, it no longer makes sense to think of parties as associations of equally empowered members having deep roots in civil society and committed to the discursive formation of opinion.

The third model likewise envisages "realistic" reforms that would bend to the pressure of media democracy's communications rules by professionalizing party communications, and even more directly and unabashedly placing them under the authority of the top-echelon communications centers staffed by experts. The only difference is that this model would still leave a place for the hard core of activist members, who would be assigned two roles. First, they would help influence the formation of public opinion in civil society by actively participating in its discussions. Second, they would continue to take part in intra-party deliberations and so shape policy positions, which, though not directly binding on the leadership, would still carry great weight with them.

Rescue for parties in Europe?

In the year 2000 the national leadership of the German SPD created a reform proposal that dovetailed with this type of "communications party" in many of its details. The plan consistently envisioned a bridging strategy designed to strengthen both the strategic communications center and the party's grass roots in civil society, while downplaying the opinion-shaping role and public profile of hierarchical, complex bodies like the party organizations and apparatus. Even though this model may have a real chance of succeeding, certain points in it have yet to be clarified. How will the nexus between the communications center and the grass roots be organized? The former puts a premium on flexibility, while the latter is thoroughly inter-twined with civil society and thus wedded to its leisurely pace of communication. Therefore, one might expect tensions, mistrust and alienation to spring up between the two levels of the party. It remains to be seen whether the internet might prove useful in defusing the potentially tense relationship inherent in this notion of how the party is supposed to work.

Comparatively speaking, parliaments have experienced an espe-cially drastic loss of influence over the political process in media democracy.[6] This is more the case for European parliamentary democracies than for presidential forms such as that of the United States, in which the president has always had a source of legitimacy separate from that of the legislative branch. The election of the chief executive in the United States has long since become a personal plebiscite conducted in the media, whereas this media-dominated process of legitimation only began to be established in the course of the nineties of the twentieth century in European parliamentary democracies. There, constitutional norms and public perceptions still treat parties and parliaments as the supreme source of legitimacy for the incumbents of the highest offices. As American and French examples have shown over a period of many decades, presidential democracies often face the dilemma of divided government. The two independent conduits of legitimacy, presidential and parliamentary elections, may produce contradictory results, which means that the president, despite his enormous powers, has to confront a hostile majority in part or all of the legislative branch. He may then be forced to enter into difficult negotiations with the leaders of the legislative majority party in order to get his program enacted into law.

Such cases generate a classic political problem of balancing con-flicts of value and interest that afflicts both the incumbent of the (directly legitimated) chief executive's office and the leadership of the majority party in one or both legislative chambers. Normally, they can only be resolved by tough bargaining backed by significant resources on a case-by-case basis. Former President Clinton, for example, faced hostile majorities in both chambers of Congress for the final six years of his tenure in office. As a result – and because of spectacular débâcles like his health-care proposal – he had to backtrack quickly or risk coming up empty in his many skirmishes with the Congress and so earning the image of a loser and a do-nothing President. His "triangulation strategy," an early variant of the third way between traditional Democratic thinking and the dogmatic anti-government rhetoric of the Republicans, was part of his response to that dilemma. Nevertheless, we should never underestimate the power of a United States president. As Clinton learned his lessons and understood better the potentialities of his office, he was able to get much of what he wanted from a Congress whose leaders did not favor him, often by threatening to veto their pet projects.

European parliamentary democracies evolved in a quite different direction partly as a result of the influence of political parties. The original notion of a legislative branch removed from and overseeing the executive was in practice supplanted by the rivalry between the government and majority party acting as a single unit arrayed against a minority opposition party (or coalition of parties). To this extent the classical model of a tripartite division of powers had long since yielded to a different reality, in which political parties bridge the gaps separating the individual pillars of the division of powers, more strongly in the case of legislative and executive power, more weakly between both of these and the judiciary. The outcome was a shift in the oversight relationship: rather than the parliament overseeing the government, now the minority opposition exercises some control over the governing majority. On account of specific parliamentary rights of oversight accorded even to the minority, this function can be exercised much more efficaciously than it might at first seem. Under these circumstances the politics of the governing majority typically emerges through a process of deliberation, consensus-building, and sometimes bargaining, between the cabinet and the leadership of the party's contingent in parliament. Depending on the political weight carried by the leading figures on each side, government representatives always tried to reach advance agreements with the chiefs of their party's parliamentary delegation, since they wanted to avoid later rumors of discord that might detract from their reputations as leaders.

In media democracy, by contrast, the marginalization of political parties has caused parliament to go into eclipse as well. The governing party's parliamentary representatives know from experience and prudential wisdom that they owe their electoral success primarily or even entirely to the media skills of their candidate for the top government post. Moreover, they realize that discrepancies between the proposals of the head of government and those of the party's parliamentary leaders only tend to diminish and eventually exhaust the former's media charisma. Therefore, they are almost always ready to work toward consensus beforehand, or even after the fact, by adopting some of the party chief's plans.

In a media democracy the head of government has planned and executed his rise to power on the assumption that such media-inspired harmonizing mechanisms will always work to his advantage. There is the chance, though, that things will go awry at some point, that a headstrong minority will not let itself be intimidated by the calculus of media-oriented strategies, or that the government's and party leaders' fondness for the media spotlight will set them at loggerheads. In this case not only political parties but also their representatives in parliament, the party contingents, will be pushed to the sidelines of the political process. And of course, given the principle of majority rule, that means that parliaments as such suffer the same fate in media democracy.[7]

This tendency is intensified still more when government leaders organize extra-parliamentary negotiations and talks designed to foster greater cooperation and consensus among major interest groups, then publicly proclaim their efforts as evidence of success in governing. The majority party contingent in parliament loses most of its room for maneuver, and is reduced to the role of auxiliary supporter of the government's policies, at most demanding minor changes in the details of initiatives sponsored by the executive. It has very little opportunity to participate in decisions that determine the broad outlines of the government's policies.

Summary

All along the line, under the pressure of media democracy all those political institutions and organizations which represent the political time concepts of long duration tend to become marginalized, while those that are able to cater directly to the needs of the media stage tend to shift to the center of the political process. Political parties may still capture public attention through their activity in local politics and their residual power to set a tone and direction for the leadership. Under the hammer of media logic, there is a tendency for the communications strategies of the party leadership to lose contact with the rank-and-file and lose patience with its snail-paced deliberations.

Traditionally, political parties played a double role in this process. On the one hand they sought to integrate particular interests into proposals that could gain society-wide support. On the other hand, when they succeeded at the polls and assumed the reins of government, they sought to implement and take responsibility for their programs. But, under the prevailing conditions of media democracy, above all the logic of its time-schedules, they are more and more pushed out to the exurbs of politics. The political process that takes place within society, one that parties once embodied and made possible, thus exchanges its erstwhile role as the primary channel of influence upon the finished product of politics, for the status of marginal player.

To be sure, parties can always adapt to the changed temporal structures, to win back lost influence in new ways. In addition to the American model, the outlines of a European model of party behavior can now be discerned. Here the parties reorganize their communicative patterns to gain influence within civil society, thus preventing their exclusion from the centers of decision-making. But the parties' weaknesses will continue to surface whenever the media communications dynamics require quick reactions to current events, and wherever the day-to-day exigencies of the national political scene demand practical implementation.

As participants in the institutional infrastructure of the long time-frame of politics in a media democracy, the intermediary sector and even parliaments also tend to lose influence and their centrality for the political process of the day. The governing party parliamentary representatives know from experience and prudential wisdom that they owe their electoral success primarily or even entirely to the media skills of their candidate for the top government post. Moreover, they realize that discrepancies between the proposals of the head of government and those of the party parliamentary leaders only tend to diminish and eventually exhaust the former's media charisma. Therefore, they are almost always ready to work toward consensus beforehand, or even after the fact, by adopting some of the party's chief plans.

Thus, the entire power structure of media democracy is increasingly different from that of the traditional European multi-party democracies. Political power tends to be embodied in the triangular recursive relation between the top political actors with media charisma, the media and permanent polling. Political deliberation and participation are losing relevance.

6

Prospects for Media Democracy

The internet: a democratic alternative?

Great expectations

Supporters of strong democracy expect a great deal of the internet, even that its technical potential might be engaged to revive a version of direct democracy characteristic of the ancient Athenian *polis*, except now on a virtual plane. Its technical infrastructure and the software required to use it seem capable of converting the old, hierarchical, one-to-many structure of communication into a new, many-to-many pattern.[1] If so, it could usher in a non-hierarchical, essentially symmetrical form of communication accessible to everyone, which could move the public sphere closer to the discursive ideal of an assembly democracy open to all citizens. Technically speaking, the net could indeed fulfil many of these expectations, and anecdotal examples abound of the net having been used to promote citizens' initiatives. These considerations have sparked hopes that the democratic deficits of media democracy might be overcome by the development of the system of mass communications itself. Allegedly, then, all diagnoses of the current malaise are merely snapshots of a moving target, the rapidly developing field of technical communications, and will be rendered obsolete in short order. So the media democracy of tomorrow, shaped by the internet, will open up a whole new world, in which the rules of the television age will lose much of their relevance.

Many observers further expect that the development of net democracy will mean the end of representative democracy in the classic mold, including especially the public character of mass communication and the deliberative and decision-making organs associated with parliamentary government and party democracy. Many internet boosters welcome the demise of these representative institutions on the grounds that they always alienated citizens from the political process anyway. By contrast, the conditions of the internet's public sphere would supposedly favor the emergence of a new constitution built on "semi-direct" democracy. Assuming such expectations are met, the new public sphere will encourage each and every citizen to take part in discussions meant to educate public opinion and guide public choice. These qualities of direct democracy will combine easily with a broadening of citizen access to and participation in central decision-making by the administration and political leadership.

New opportunities and risks

Advances in technology do indeed offer participants in the internet's political communications forums almost unlimited opportunities for flexible, self-determined interaction, free from the traditional boundaries of social class and physical space. Experts therefore say it is only a question of time before this renewed qualitative leap in the structural transformation of the public sphere ushers in a new form of democracy. They predict that the classic institutions of representative and party democracy will wither away, while opportunities for democratic participation and decision-making will multiply dramatically for most citizens. This line of argument is reinforced by the fact that the net also furnishes almost unlimited prospects for combining the dissemination of political information with actual political participation, thus eventually permitting all citizens so inclined to have a say in whatever affairs most deeply concerned them.

From this perspective the mediacratic power structures of the twenty-first century appear as little more than a transitional phase. On the horizon beckons a utopia of domination-free communications, in which the selection and representation rules of the mass media would become irrelevant, as would the obsession of today's political actors with bestriding media-generated stages. But objections can be raised against this optimistic scenario for democratic renewal on four different planes: society and culture, mass culture, communications theory, and socio-economic conditions. These reservations mutually reinforce one another. Their impact, plus a few years of experience with the internet and opportunities to reflect on its practical implications, have largely muted the once euphoric expectations of proponents. Nevertheless, they do still leave room for hope that the net might one day enhance the prospects of democracy.

New problems and challenges

Addressing the socio-cultural problematic, Umberto Eco has predicted that the expansion of internet access will lead to a new kind of class division unparalleled in its rigidity (the digital divide). In all likelihood a considerable number of people will lack the skills and willingness to develop basic competence in the use of network communications. Limited competence and interest in the net, as well as economic barriers to purchasing the necessary equipment, will accentuate in the long term the trend toward a two-class society of users and non-users. It is already apparent in all countries and may result in a permanent social divisions along these lines. Those who are already well-informed about and intensively involved in political affairs will only enhance both of these advantages by adroit use of the net and thereby put even more distance between themselves and the rest of society. Much could be said in favor of Eco's conclusions. A comparison of network user-groups in European countries shows that those who use it most are precisely the young, well-educated, high-income professionals who tend to work in cutting-edge fields, and who already understand how to maintain their independence from the old mass media, while enjoying them actively. By contrast, the internet is still an alien world for those strata – not necessarily older people – who are politically and socially passive, attracted exclusively to the products of mass culture, with relatively lower levels of income and education. For the first group internet use turns out to enhance the advantages they already possess by virtue of their social engagements and active utilization of the mass media. It offers them additional information, new opportunities to communicate, and a way to bring the whole world into their homes or offices. For the second group, the disadvantages that already weigh them down are magnified. Already excluded from many other socio-cultural domains, they now find themselves locked out of the newest and most versatile medium of all.

On the socio-economic level, another objection can be raised against internet optimism, one that supports Eco's predictions about an emergent two-track society. The high cost of acquiring the technical equipment (both hard- and software) needed for the net may continue to pose an insuperable barrier for lower-income strata. Moreover, it takes a great deal of time to obtain all this equipment and acquire sufficient computer literacy to use it with some prospect of success and personal benefit. In the long run a great many people will find themselves shut out of the net by one or the other of these hurdles.

On the plane of mass culture we can observe a widespread tendency for the older media to colonize the new ones. The editors of newspapers and radio stations have successfully invested major resources to place their products on the internet, where they are used in more or less the same way as in the classic mass media. Besides that, the net is literally swamped by overt or covert commercial entertainment As a result its interactivity and symmetry, the true sources of its technical potential and the basis of the hopes reposed in it, have been overshadowed amid the greater number of commercial sites. There are many indications that these trends will not weaken but intensify in the future. So it is reasonable to expect that, from now on, the internet will be used predominantly as a new technical system for distributing old-fashioned mass communications content. In political contexts, as much US research indicates, the net tends to be used as an additional means of communication by previously existing social and political networks.[2] Alternatively, it stimulates the formation of new, rather narrow groupings built around specific special interests (virtual balkanization).

On the level of communications theory critics charge that the internet tends largely to privatize the political public sphere, since individuals can only tap its potential in isolation. In this way internet chatrooms, for example, can avoid the opinion-filtering effects encouraged by traditional representative public life and communications among participants who are present in the same physical location. Even when conversations in the interactive zone of net communications include many people, they still have the air of exchanges between private persons. What is missing is the opportunity for the individual to emerge from the private sphere into a public space, and join in discussions guided by the special rules regulating discourse about public affairs. Robert Putnam has summarized the results of numerous empirical studies on this tendency in two succinct claims. First, "virtual" social capital, which is not based on tight, enduring relationships among people who are physically present together, is a contradiction in terms. Second, in the absence of social pressure to be civil, internet communications often degenerate into vicious attack campaigns ("flaming out").

All of these criticisms are justified, but only to rein in overdrawn expectations. They do not defuse the main argument, that the internet does in principle offer new possibilities for democratic communications. In particular, there are four dimensions in which it can expand the scope of democratic communication and action, although it can never supercede the dominant role of mass-media communication. First, the net dramatically enhances the access activist groups will have to internal information from various institutions and the centers of political decision-making. The internet can be used directly or indirectly to set up independent group initiatives, or as the starting-point for intervening in politics along more traditional lines. In either case, the net multiplies opportunities for political participation.

Second, the internet has already proven to be an efficacious instrument for organizing local and regional citizens' action networks in civil society, as shown by the student strikes in Germany during the summer semester of 1997. Without the net to establish liaisons among the strikers' headquarters at different universities, the strike would never have happened. When authoritarian political leaders impose communications blockades, the internet can also provide a forum for transmitting information, exchanging opinion, and coordinating specific protests that central authorities cannot easily control. As the opposition rallies in Serbia during 1998/99 proved, the net can be a highly effective substitute for the public communications that political authorities have barred from the stage offered by the traditional media. Finally, activist internet communities can put neglected public issues on the mass media's agenda, and thus make political actors aware of them as well. This is how coverage of the Clinton–Lewinsky scandal started, after the establishment media had ignored it. In numerous European nations new social movements used unusual forms of communication in civil society to impose their agenda on the traditional media and ultimately on national-level politics. In the same way activist internet communities can influence the media's mode of communication and eventually public policy, provided they choose issues suited to the new medium.

Factual options

An empirically sound, sober assessment of the internet's potential to enhance democratic communication should not encourage those who are expecting it to usher in a new age of democracy. But, all things considered, there are good reasons to believe that it may broaden the scope of democratic communication and action by supplementing already existing channels. Both its technical potential and its use by dissidents in civil society and politics inspire long-term confidence. The mass media will continue to dominate the public sphere in spite of the internet, but their hegemony may be noticeably reduced and qualified. That may be especially true for political dictatorships, in which the net can reopen blocked or prohibited channels of public discussion. But it holds for functioning democracies as well, since the internet may improve the prospects of citizens' lobbies in civil society to get action taken on their grievances and force the mass media to take up issues that they would prefer to avoid.

It remains to be seen whether more broad-gaged, intensive inter-net use will stimulate a tendency that is already quite marked: the fragmentation of the public sphere into a series of partial publics. If experience is any guide, those who make a point of participating actively or passively in the main forums of the public sphere, will probably do the same with the internet's selection of topics and opportunities for discourse. So we should not expect that they will turn their backs on those traditional forums simply because they are attracted by the possibilities of internet communication. On the other hand, those who even today skirt the margins of the wider public sphere, because their interests focus narrowly on certain kinds of mass-media offerings (specific topics, regions, fields, or clienteles), will probably follow the same pattern on the internet. The many people who derive the bulk of their political information and judg-ments from watching or reading entertainment fare would in any case be among the group with the least access to the internet anyway. And even if they did have such access, they would probably do what they already do: browse in search of entertainment features. In short, the internet is unlikely to change the habits of most user-groups, but instead reinforce the tendencies they have already shown in their response to the more traditional public sphere.

There is, however, one important democratic deficit that the inter-net may exacerbate, involving the role of dialogue and consensus-oriented deliberation as an element of public life. Members of new, highly individualized, and well-educated strata have maintained a marked interest in politics while evincing great skepticism toward political parties. There are indications that their desire to reach rational and well-informed political choices will drive them away from participation in the traditional forums of civil society, which rely on public discussions among people who are physically present in the same place. Instead, they may opt for the network's inter-active, "virtual" communications. It can offer them a great deal that civil society cannot: easier access, a greater degree of autonomy, choice of times, topics, and partners, freedom from any specific meeting place and agenda, and the attraction of mastering the new medium's immense technical potential.

When groups, whose members already know one another from other social and political settings and "real-life" meetings, engage in virtual conferencing that should not pose any inherent threat to stan-dards of democratic deliberation. But if all or most communications were to shift to the net, then their quality would be essentially altered. Time-lagged communications among individual persons operating out of anonymous private spaces would replace the consensus-oriented deliberations of people assembled together in a public space. The presence of others exercises a kind of social control; it forces the participants to clarify their arguments and imposes certain responsibilities on the speaker. By contrast, internet chatrooms are notoriously full of racist statements and ungrounded, dogmatic accusations and assertions that their authors would never dare utter in a traditional public setting. Thus the preconditions, the proceed-ings, and the consequences of communication all undergo ominous changes.

Balancing democratic gains and losses

Scanell has argued that we have to strike an overall positive balance concerning the relationship between public broadcasting and democ-racy. According to him broadcasting as a public good has unobtru-sively contributed to the democratization of everyday life. It does this through asserting a right of access to public life for every citizen and through questioning those in power on behalf of viewers and listeners.[3] Corner has raised the objection that this positive balance needs some correction in the light of the increasing influence of com-mercial broadcasting in the public sphere.[4] In this section I will argue that Scannell's argument deserves even more substantial correction regarding the changes the new mix of commercial and private broadcasting has prompted in the key areas of politics itself: politi-cal participation and decision-making.

More direct democracy?

In analyzing the structure of political power in media democracy, we should be especially attentive to the continuing connection between the most up-to-date poll results and the media-oriented trial balloons floated by political elites. Some have considered it a victory for democracy that the "voice of the people" now enters directly and distortion-free into the inner councils of politics. The intermediary bodies of deliberative democracy, the associations, interest groups and parties that once transmitted political demands and consensus, can finally be bypassed. Specifically, politics in media democracy has two ways of circumventing the intermediary system: the populist method and the corporatist strategy.

Media democracy and the populist method   Neither ancient nor modern republics have ever legitimated democracy exclusively through voting and majority rule. The political role of the public sphere has been an equally significant, perhaps even more funda-mental source of legitimacy, especially in light of the implicit claim democracy makes to be a form of rule superior to rival models. The notion of the public sphere most relevant to democracy always contained an implicitly normative claim in both its ancient and modern European variants. Proposals and alternatives, claims and critiques were not only supposed to be public in the sense of "pub-licly known" or "promulgated." Rather, both systems of democratic legitimation assumed a qualitative conception of the public sphere, one in which political claims were to be scrutinized rationally by all concerned.

This model of the public sphere tacitly presupposed a unitary structure of social time and space. The public sphere was understood as a social space in which citizens – i.e., all those entitled to take part in political decision-making – were brought together in a nexus of rational communication, whether in an active or passive role. There were at least two good reasons for the presumption of a unitary, seamless flow of time in which public communication could proceed. First, it allowed ideas and proposals to mature gradually and be exposed to scrutiny. And, second, it gave the public a chance to consult its experiences with its elected representatives, especially to see whether their actions in office dovetailed with what they had previously advocated in public debates, and thus whether they possessed the personal integrity and credibility to deserve a new mandate. In this sense votes were judgments about previously held discussions.

By contrast, the political process of media democracy interrogates the incipient, momentary preferences of isolated citizens, making them the point of departure for entire media strategies. People's initially fluid, inchoate opinions are thus reinforced and stabilized.[5] There is no time or space for public deliberation that would allow a well-founded public opinion to emerge, and, as a result, the public sphere relinquishes two of its previously constitutive functions in a democracy: validating opinions and providing political orientation. Under the aegis of the populist strategy the apparently more direct contact between the leadership and the populace ends up yielding a loss of democratic control.

The corporatist strategy   We need to consider a second version of the hypothesis that the marginalization of parties will actually strengthen democracy in media-dominated societies. It focuses on the tendency for systems of consensus to emerge among the interests and associations in society without the involvement of political parties. By the logic of this argument, a corporatist consensus among the strongest social and economic interest groups and associations – excluding the parties – proves the most democratic road to legitimacy, assuming the consensus is effectively presented in the media. It invokes the direct participation and consent of societal actors, rather than relying on the mediating role of parties and parliament. The key premise of this argument, then, is that the procedures and substance of decisions will be most democratic if societal interests can be translated as directly as possible into political decisions, "eliminating the middleman" as it were.

Seen in this light, the very presence of parties – their organizations, *modus operandi* and role as mediating links in parliamentary democracy – seems to betoken an erosion of democracy. In comparison, legitimation via public relations begins to look like a plus for democracy. Taken to its logical conclusion, this would mean calling any regime a "grass-roots" media democracy in which the state bargained with interest-group representatives and knew how to sell the results successfully in the media. If we understand democracy this way, we will inevitably see the system of intermediary political organizations as an unnecessary detour, because of the way these groups aggregate interests, transmit them among one another and to the political system, and constantly consult with their constituencies about the outcomes of the process.

There are good arguments that can be adduced in support of this position. First, in terms of the theory of democracy and actual democratic politics, few would wish to deny the validity of the subsidiarity principle. If smaller social units can manage their own affairs by way of deliberation and consensus, then they ought to do so. Not only would they be honoring the rules of democratic legitimacy; they would actually be improving on them, certainly far more than would be the case if higher authorities arrogated all such decisions to themselves, as though they were tutelary powers. At least this is true as long as those directly affected arrive at a consensus voluntarily, and are not coerced into giving their consent by pressure, dependency or the blandishments of money. There is another case in which direct societal negotiations seem to insure a higher order of democracy: namely, when all those who would potentially be affected by a decision have a chance to participate in it, and the agreed-upon settlement does not adversely affect third parties excluded from the process. Communitarians find these sorts of arrangements especially appealing, both in their theoretical writings and in their practical recommendations. The idea does seem plausible that negotiations among societal actors where the state acts as moderator signify a twofold gain for democracy. On the one hand, the reach of centralized bureaucracies is restricted; on the other – and in equal measure – those directly concerned in decisions have more influence on them.

This model of course comes up against its limits when the interests of excluded parties have to be taken into account. It will not do to claim that their interests are automatically represented merely because agents of the state are involved. After all, the linkage between interests and policy is exactly what has all along given political parties their claim to legitimacy. Their very *raison d'être*, their functional imperative, has been to process and aggregate the interests of society into platforms capable of gaining majority support in the democratic process. Thereafter, they are expected to implement, adhere to and take full public responsibility for the interest-aggregating programs they defended during elections. The state in its persona as broker or mediator simply cannot claim the same degree of legitimacy as a party that has emerged victorious from an election with a clear mandate to govern.

Social consensus politics that bypasses parties and relies on the media for legitimation can only be justified as pro-democracy to the extent that it respects its own boundaries and recognizes that unrepresented third parties have a stake in decisions. Otherwise, although it may sometimes generate acceptable outcomes and even lead to the inclusion of major interest groups, its democratic credentials will always be suspect. Democratic institutions are not just an accessory that drags out and formalizes decision-making processes. Rather, they establish procedures and guarantee that the political programs debated in elections will eventually receive the consent of the governed following their full and fair participation. It hardly makes sense to speak of gains for democracy when a few key actors achieve a consensus that touches the interests of society as a whole, and then seek external support for it by presenting it cleverly in the media, even though their consensus does not reflect the will of the parties. The truth is that the authority to make decisions has not been shifted back to "society" at all, but instead to a club of the most powerful elites who decide for everybody else. The problem for democratic politics is not whether the societal actors involved in an issue have reached their decisions with or without state participation, but rather that they proclaim the legitimacy of their decisions for the whole society in and through the media, without using the appropriate democratic procedures. In short, there is no basis in democratic theory for the claim that media democracy offers a more direct route to popular influence on decisions by circumventing the parties.

Infotainment and information

Trends toward depoliticization

Pippa Norris, in her cross-national study, has concluded – on the basis of comparing institutional structures of national media systems with the distribution of practical political knowledge in these countries – that empirical evidence cannot sustain the mediamalaise hypothesis, according to which the faculty of political judgment is disintegrating under the impact of the mass media.[6] However, in-depth studies in the structure of civics knowledge have yielded quite different results. These investigations show that both media fare itself (excepting high-quality print media) and the consciousness of the broad public have suffered declines: citizens are less well-informed and less able to make political judgments now than they once were.[7] Our own empirical studies of the political content of television programs and print media do not justify any statements about developments over time, but they do permit clear judgments about the present. Even in overtly political television broadcasts there is a preponderance of programming with extremely scanty informational content and little room for debate, with much of it offering an image of the political that would more likely distract viewers from actual events than help them understand what has been happening. The most crucial informational inputs emanating from an important segment of the mass-media system, in short, simply do not meet the standards of appropriate information for a democratic polity. Some researchers, like Eliasoph, would locate the primary motives for politics avoidance in the citizens' life-world, whereas the mediamalaise theorists would blame it on the media system itself.[8] Regardless of who or what is responsible, we must recognize that, in this respect, the input of the media system does suffer from a serious "deficit."

It is not so much that political media communications necessarily or inherently condemn political realities to underexposure and distortion. Yet these failings are in fact abetted by modern media practices. Low production costs (achieved by miserly research expenditures) and guarantees of high viewer interest put a premium on the kind of programs that do distort the political.

Empirical studies have likewise shown that it is always possible in any medium to develop appropriate, sophisticated political programming. The media are all too happy to subsume politics and its personnel under their own production values, which as previously noted emphasize vacuous rules of attention-getting and entertainment elements. There is yet in fact no necessary causal link between the dominance of electronic mass media, with their inescapable pre-production standards, and the informational void that afflicts political reportage. Empirical content analysis of the way the media construct the political instead suggest that their stage-management techniques do not raise insuperable barriers to depicting political issues appropriately, i.e., with a reasonable level of information and editorial commentary.[9] It is certainly true that the media stage is a sham political reality. But the problem consists in the sham, not the staging, which suggests that radical cultural critiques of the sort written by Neil Postman are unfounded.[10]

Stage-management and rationality

The most recent research has tended to confirm the hypothesis that, given the current state of the mass media, it would be inappropriate to draw any a priori distinction between entertainment and information. Morley and Dahlgren in particular have highlighted the positive contributions that journalistic popular culture can make in communicating the political and making it understandable.[11] Pursuing one aspect of this process, audience research has demonstrated that such successful communication depends on the receptivity of the media users themselves. But in this study I want to investigate a rather more neglected question: what qualities of the mass-media products themselves have to be enhanced for us to judge the synthesis of entertainment and information as a success? The most extreme form of the constructivist thesis cannot be regarded as empirically well-founded. In its supply-oriented version it denies that there is any way to evaluate media constructions objectively, since every attempt at an evaluation would just turn out to be another new construction. And in its demand-oriented version it maintains that the proffered texts themselves are simply irrelevant, since it is after all the recipients alone, in their polysemic nature, who must make sense of them. But if we go along with the assumption of Hall and Morley that the preferred media text does indeed have a considerable influence on the way a relevant segment of the public will assimilate it, then certain consequences for democratic theories and commitments must follow. We must inquire how well media texts, staged mainly for their entertainment value, manage to meet the conditions for an adequate rendering of political information. I propose that only some kinds of entertainment-oriented media texts should be regarded as appropriate for conveying political information and as beneficial in terms of democratic theory: namely, those in which the dimensions and factors of political logic in a given state-of-affairs remain sufficiently discernible.

Accordingly, the logic of the political itself must be the criterion for evaluating the appropriateness of media syntheses between entertainment and information. Appropriate syntheses of this kind are possible, and can be seen or heard every day in the mass media, even on television. However, they are the exception rather than the rule, as empirical research can confirm.

Politics staged for the media has certain things in common with other aesthetic products: it implicitly claims to portray its subject-matter authentically and truthfully, and it employs a polyvalent linguistic and non-linguistic sign system across all genres. But political productions differ from most others by striving to represent something that existed prior to its having been staged, an external event amenable to intersubjective scrutiny. They therefore embody a mixed type of rationality in terms of Habermas's theory of communications.[12] They contain elements of aesthetic expression, as well as validity claims concerning the truth of the information provided and the correctness of arguments made about it.

Thus media stage-management of politics does make implicit claims to rationality. Within broad limits it permits information to be adduced concerning political issues and, to a lesser extent, features the repartee of argument and counter-argument. Furthermore, there is no reason to doubt that the media can provide complete, accurate information while at the same time indulging in various degrees and kinds of stage-management. The two activities are not mutually exclusive. We might suggest a comparison between media productions of politics and pedagogy. For didactic purposes, skilled teachers may choose to simplify the topic in question to make it accessible to the non-experts they instruct, although these simplifications should not trivialize the topic. Certain forms of media-staging may likewise produce a synthesis that transforms the subject-matter without compromising the integrity of its informational core. Infotainment is not the enemy of information *per se*. In fact its commitment to entertainment, drama, and emotional involvement may open up access routes to the domain of political affairs that would otherwise remain closed to many people. After all, attracting attention to themes of common interest and presenting them accurately is precisely the social function of the mass media. The question that has stirred the most critical comment from partisans of democratic politics is whether the mass media's attention-getting devices enthrall the audience at the price of distorting the essential reality of what they are trying to present, folding it into a stage-managed simulacrum. The temptation to do this resides in the opportunity structure of the media system itself, since as a rule the mass public will tolerate attractively staged productions, even if they are practically devoid of content.

The deficiency of generalized cultural criticism à la Postman is its refusal to draw a clear distinction between the way that media-staging rules work in principle, and the way they are typically handled by commercial media executives in their day-to-day business decisions. It is based on the empirically refuted premise that the temptation to

distort, which is immanent in the media's opportunity structure, con-
stitutes the one and only determining factor in the way such decisions
are reached. But there is a world of difference between these two phe-
nomena. The vapid productions of the mass media may in fact only
define what political communication is now, not what it could become
under more favorable circumstances. On the other hand, as long as the
mass media continue running the show, there may be no chance
in principle for any alternative, more appropriate manner of staging
politics to emerge. In the latter case the only way to find a public
sphere committed to a modicum of informative reportage and rationality would be to seek it outside the media. But in the former case, it
would just be a matter of pushing the envelope of the current media
system, using it better, more deliberately, and more responsibly. The
task of democracy's proponents would then be to heighten the prob-
ability that the media will live up to its responsibilities. This could be
achieved most readily if self-governing professional organizations and
civil-society watchdog groups cooperated to set standards for guiding
media communications more efficaciously.

Broad leeway for adequate information

The decisive question, then, concerns how media-system actors themselves use the leeway afforded them when they effect a synthesis of
aesthetics and facts. How do they apply the rules that inescapably
limit their choices, and how do they balance both claims in their
productions: the law of attracting attention versus the imperative of
accuracy in the contexts of reporting? There are four crucial factors
that determine the success of such syntheses, listed in ascending
order of their importance.

First, media actors must acquire competence in two areas in order
to master the rules of both elements in the synthesis. Specifically, they
need to understand the special logic of the political as well as the
techniques of media stage-management. Second, they should have the
will, competence and sense of responsibility to measure the success
of their work not by the usual media standard (attracting attention),
but by how well they have managed to synthesize both desiderata.
Third, what really matters in institutions is the economy of time. Only
when there is enough time available to do research and work on
creating a synthesis is it likely to succeed. Experienced professionals
can stir up a *mélange* of emotional effects into an instant media production in a New York minute. But doing careful research on the

contexts of the story and turning it into a media product that does justice to them requires a good bit more time and spadework. Fourth, as in any other profession so too in this one: it is primarily media professionals who formulate quality standards and keep up the pressure on one another to produce superior work. A culture of democratic responsibility in editorial offices, if need be buttressed by an attentive public sphere, can undergird high standards of journalistic integrity in the media. What largely determines the quality level of media content, then, is the communicative culture that surrounds the media, particularly the efforts of societal actors to enforce high standards.

Civil society and the media

The relevance of extra-media communication

Political communications that affect decision-making are never restricted to what is created for or appears in the mass media, even in a media democracy. Communicative processes are always going on, if nowhere else at least in the centers of political action within civil society, in parliamentary working groups and the executive branch, where preliminary discussions pave the way for later decisions.[13] Although participants in these processes never lose sight of the potential media-worthiness of their communications, the latter are not usually media-oriented as they transpire. Political communication as negotiation and consensus-oriented deliberation does occur on many levels in media democracy, but it fails to get noticed by the general public precisely because it shuns the media stage and does not put its stamp on the public sphere. Besides political communications external to the media, we should not fail to mention politics as rule- and law-making, an activity that takes place on every echelon of decision-making. In addition to legislation, it would also include administrative regulations intended to implement political programs in a variety of areas from education and internal security to research, economic policy, welfare, and defense.

The argument that politics is being absorbed into its media productions thus overstates the case and loses touch with reality, despite having identified a genuinely worrisome trend. The political public sphere is in fact on the verge of becoming a house of mirrors, in which both politics and the media recognize only images of themselves, thereby losing sight of the real world. But life goes on behind the mirrors, in the life-worlds of ordinary citizens as well as in the antechambers and control centers of power. To an unparalleled extent power and the logic of its deployment, use and effects are withdrawing behind the scenes of the media. At first glance they elude us. Yet the media can escape from the house of mirrors if they refuse to accept the stage-managed scenarios the political world offers them. Instead, they should pay attention to the logic of political processes, although admittedly stage-managed events do constitute a good portion of the political realities in today's media societies. Even in media democracy one can find genuine politics understood as the process of making binding decisions that follow political rather than media logic. It can still be observed behind the scenes of the media stage, though the powers that direct the stage personae have given the whole process a new look.

Deep effects of media communication

The reach of the media is practically unlimited in the political process, affecting expectations, power struggles, cost estimates, and the selection of topics, personnel and timing. When political elites try to stage-manage their own media exposure, their gamesmanship would appear to empty politics of all content. But inside these illusions there remains a hard core of genuine politics, i.e., strategic action aimed at gaining or maintaining legitimate power. In this sense political elites are promoting their own professional interests when they elaborately stage-manage appearances. Yet they make all their efforts under the pressure and according to the rules of the media system, so politics remains a colonized province rather than the autonomous author of its own logic. It surrenders to the conditions set by the media, involuntarily undermining any chance it might have to show the wider public all of its idiosyncrasies and limitations, the conditions affecting political action and accomplishment. On the media stage politics makes its entrance in borrowed costumes. Politicians see how crudely and incompetently they are portrayed in media productions, mostly due to the political ignorance of journalists, always under such pressure to maximize ratings. As a result political actors resolve to assume responsibility for staging their own media appearances, hoping at least to define the message that is being disseminated as much as they can. Declining political competence in the media reinforces the politicians' confidence in their own stage-management skills. And so begins the vicious circle of media democracy. In the end politics cannot risk appearing without disguises for fear that people will take it for an unpleasant and inscrutable caricature of what the media had customarily portrayed it to be. Paradoxically, the media image of politics predisposes the public to judge it in the light of non-political criteria. From the vantage point of democratic theory the question arises: how can this downward spiral be checked? Jürgen Habermas, in reflecting on the theoretical principles of his *Structural Transformation of the Public Sphere*, has found cause in recent political developments to rethink that book's pessimistic conclusions.[14] For instance, he has pointed out the twofold advantages of the civic forums of civil society. On occasion they function as alternative public spheres capable of effecting positive – albeit only temporary – changes in the state of the wider media-dominated public sphere. Furthermore, a deliberative public sphere emerges in the forums of civil society as they work toward building consensus about matters of common concern. If they make a sustained and broad-gaged effort, the forums may spur the media to consider topics their filter systems would long since have blocked out. Moreover, they can insist that the mass media provide a higher standard of information and editorial comment in its treatment of these topics than the media's production routines would normally permit. Consensus-oriented deliberation as practiced in the forums of civil society raises public awareness. When a politicized public makes emphatic, high-profile demands, it can extract concessions even from television networks in respect to topics and modes of communication that will be aired. The emergence of the so-called new social movements in the seventies and eighties in many European countries lends support to Habermas's revision of the theory of mass-media communications.

Split public spheres

Partisans of democracy in the media age thus have reason to place their hopes in the forums of civil society and the political commitments of ordinary citizens, for they seem able to slow the downward spiral in which attractive but superficial programming stage-managed by the media and political elites robs politics of all content. But there is a second reason for hope as well. Habermas himself emphasized that truth-oriented conversations among the denizens of the life-world do more than merely build consensus on issues of common concern. The social act of trying to reach consensus by deliberation also generates social cohesion or solidarity. Or, more accurately, by virtue of their social cooperation the participants maintain and rejuvenate the bonds of solidarity that such cooperation always pre-supposes. But as Robert Putnam has shown, wherever media communications, especially television, predominate, there are bound to be some adverse psychological and social consequences. The well-springs that continually replenish energies of social cohesion may run dry, and citizens' willingness to make social and civic commitments may falter. To be sure, media communication does generate para-social fictions. It seems to the viewers as though they are entering into social relationships, ones that TV personages apparently reciprocate. But such fictions obviously can never replace the forms of social coop-eration that really generate social cohesion, since no true reciprocal exchange between persons is taking place. Instead, they isolate the person and weaken his or her motivation to take part in the conversations of the life-world. Besides, the pseudo-sociability of television takes up a lot of time that might otherwise be devoted to civic and social commitments.

Thus, excessive television watching undermines the socio-cultural foundations of democracy in several ways, most seriously – from the point of view of democratic theory – by attacking civil society's capac-ity to act politically. Civil society is the one sphere from which might emerge forces of social opposition capable of responsibly overseeing the media system. Yet the latter markedly weakens those capacities by luring the individual out of the common life-world and into the isolation of the living-room. Of course these research findings, like most others from the field of media studies, need to be refined. Those who spend most of their time exclusively watching entertainment shows are much more likely than other viewers to fall into the syn-dromes of apathy and isolation we have just described. By contrast, viewers who mix entertainment with information shows, and certainly those who read high-quality print media, have no trouble making political or social commitments. Besides, transactional ana-lysis indicates that the content of media programming is only one of many factors that must be taken into account when we attempt to measure its effects. Prior information, motivation and concentration levels among media-users are just as significant in determining what they will finally make of the fare they consume. It is true that knowl-edgeable, highly motivated media-users can extract relevant and "correct" information from almost any media fare in conjunction with all the other shows they watch and articles they read. This is especially the case when they discuss the topics in several different contexts, with friends and colleagues, and in the social and political associations they frequent. Yet it is likewise true that a majority of citizens get nearly all their political information from television programs, though in Europe TV is often supplemented by tabloid newspapers. And these citizens often belong to the group of "swing" voters that frequently tips the scales in close elections. Thus, the virtuous effects of intensive media use must in the first instance be credited to the politically motivated and critical users and not to the media as such.

Dahlgren is certainly correct in saying that civil society alone can be expected to stimulate both a renewal of the mass media in the direction of more appropriate reporting and the emergence of other complementary forms of public communication.[15] Though one might surmise that his argument is contradicted by the finding that the intermediary political system has been marginalized, such is not the case. First of all, civil society is not coterminous with the intermediary system, since the latter also includes powerful economic lobbies and interest groups, which are not an inherent part of civil society. Second, the marginalizing of the intermediary sector, as observed under current conditions, simply means that it has been displaced from the core zones of influence over the political system. Civil society's functions as a counter-public and as a communitarian field of action remain unaffected by this trend. Third, the tendency for the intermediary sphere to be marginalized should certainly not be interpreted in a rigidly deterministic manner. Under suitable circumstances, civil society can considerably enhance its influence on the larger society and even on the political system. The current renaissance of civil society in Europe suggests that it is by no means unrealistic to harbor such expectations.

Engagement in the intermediary bodies of civil society gives active and potentially active citizens their best chance to acquire adequate political information and develop sound political judgment. Once they have these prerequisites, they will be in a position to make good use of almost any media programming they encounter. For example, follow-up conversations in civil society may help them clarify what a particular report or show means for them, and how best to evaluate it. In civil society they can likewise conduct conversations oriented to building consensus among the participants. They can form autonomous judgments and then take an active part in influencing the opinions of other members of the community. For these active citizens a given media offering is often just the first step in the process of reaching judgments about themes and ideas; nevertheless, it is a formative, defining first step. For the politically passive and apathetic segment of the audience, on the other hand, the bits and pieces of information they glean almost in passing from entertainment shows are just about all they will ever learn as they try to form judgments about politics, policies, persons, organizations and processes. This is why it must be considered as a confusion of cause and effect to credit the media instead of the active citizens when there occurs after all a virtuous circle between media reception and political activism.

And, as Habermas and Melucci have both shown, persistent initiatives emanating from civil society, although they may have limited time-horizons and focus on narrowly defined topics, can challenge the media code itself.[16] They do so by modifying the way in which syntheses between the rules of success within media logic and political logic are carried through, even in the inner sanctums of the mass-media system. In this sense one can say that within media democracy the mass-media system recognizes two distinct aggregate conditions. There is business as usual as described in this book, but there is also a "high alert" state, which can arise when a mobilized civil society actively besieges the media system. In the latter case, civil society does indeed challenge the media code, demanding an application of the media's filter system that is more appropriate to politics, without getting rid of it altogether. As a rule this high alert state will then have repercussions for the political system, partially liberating it from the constraints of colonization by the media system. Only if civil society is permanently mobilized on a broad range of issues, should we expect an effective reversal of the current trends.

Summary

Supporters of strong democracy expect a great deal of the internet, even that its technical potential might be engaged to revive a version of direct democracy characteristic of the ancient Athenian *polis*, except now on a virtual plane. Its technical infrastructure and the software required to use it seem capable of converting the old, hierarchical, one-to-many structure of communication into a new, many-to-many pattern. If so, it could usher in a non-hierarchical form of political deliberation and compensate for the deficiencies of TV-dominated media democracy.

Critics charge that the internet tends largely to privatize the political public sphere, since individuals can only tap its potential in isolation. In this way internet chatrooms, for example, can avoid the opinion-filtering effects encouraged by traditional representative public life and communications among participants who are present in the same physical location. In that sense the internet seems to have the potential to intensify some of the problems of media democracy. It is, however, too soon to predict how the different effects of the internet will influence the emerging media democracy.

Though media democracy tends to include unprecedentedly large audiences in the process of political communication, it cannot be credited with enhancing the quality of democracy. From a democratic point of view it has, in its present stage of development, three inherent weaknesses: first, it tends to put a premium on issueless stage-management; second, it tends to reify the momentary preferences of isolated citizens, making them the point of departure for professional media strategies. People's initially fluid, inchoate opinions are thus reinforced and stabilized, so that there is no time or space for public deliberation that would allow a well-founded public opinion to emerge. Third, by sidelining political parties and the intermediary sector organizations, medias democracy tends to diminish the capacity of the political system to generate citizen's participation.

However, there is enough scope for communicative appropriateness in the opportunity structure of the media stage, that it could serve as a starting-point for enhancing the democratic quality of media democracy. Critically acclaimed TV magazines, talk-shows and news coverage offer proof that, at their best, political productions in the media can achieve a synthesis on their own terms between media aesthetics and the inherent logic of the political affairs they portray.

A new culture of democratic responsibility in editorial offices, if need be buttressed by an attentive public sphere in civil society, can undergird high standards of journalistic integrity in the media. What largely determines the quality level of media content, then, is the communicative culture that surrounds the media, particularly the efforts of societal actors to enforce high standards. Consensus-oriented deliberation as practised in the forums of civil society can raise public awareness. When a politicized public makes emphatic, high-profile demands, it can extract concessions even from television networks in respect to topics that will be aired and modes of communication.

To insure that media democracy remains democracy, and only secondarily lapses into media-oriented pseudo-politics, society needs to exercise oversight and control over the media system and its mode of political communication. We recommend the notion of appropriateness to designate the overriding objective that regulation should pursue at all levels and for all products. A culture of more appropriate political communication could heighten the pressure against issueless stage-management and keep the avenues open for political participation.

Conclusion: Democracy in Transition

An open-ended process

What media democracy may have in store for European societies is not easy to foresee, but it certainly appears to be a contradictory political arrangement. Its constraints and potentialities can be plotted onto a field with two coordinates. On one hand, it inducts great masses of people into a single system of communication (the national or global village), while simultaneously depoliticizing many previously political aspects of their lives. On the other, it opens up new and attractive possibilities to enhance individual participation in the political public sphere, and open up politics to greater numbers of people. The development of media democracy in the United States may prefigure the direction it will soon take in Europe under the irresistible pressure of the rules that govern the media's version of public life. Yet the traditions of political culture in Europe, the will to self-preservation of the major political parties, and the prominence of the prestige media in the process of public communication raise doubts at this point about whether European democracies will ever converge on the American model.

Whether or not this convergence is occurring, it is clear from qualitative indices that major European democracies have already begun to operate according to the rules of media democracy. The media system's power to mold the political culture evidently far surpasses the latter's influence on the practices of the media system. The pressure political elites feel to stage-manage their media images is constant and unrelenting. Meanwhile, any hopes elected officials might have of changing the media's communicative and consumer culture on behalf of discursive politics remain uncertain and long term. So, for the foreseeable future political culture will probably have tough sledding. Nevertheless, the media's rules of selecting and presenting programming do not form a rigidly deterministic framework. That is, they do not in principle exclude other logics and points of view, nor do they operate merely as a self-enclosed system of rules.

To insure that media democracy remains democracy, and only secondarily lapses into media-oriented pseudo-politics, society needs to exercise oversight and control over the media system and its mode of political communication. It is worth making a strong recommendation for the notion of appropriateness to designate the overriding objective that regulation should pursue at all levels and for all products. The term derives from the doctrine of rhetoric in classical antiquity, which envisaged a harmony of logos, ethos, and pathos (discursive thought, an ethic of habit, and emotion). The notion of appropriateness would have to be redefined to take account of the mode of image production in politics and the media that modern communications societies have called forth. A new definition would have to incorporate the rhetoric and theatricality of the mass media. But to develop practicable criteria for assessing the appropriateness of political productions for the media stage, we cannot merely conjure up clever armchair definitions; instead, we should rely on a societal process that includes a great many participants and stakeholders. This task – democratizing the rules of media selection and presentation – may be the single greatest challenge that democratic politics will face in the future. The character and quality of democracy hinge on whether it is handled successfully.

Scope for appropriateness

The idea of appropriateness used here presumes that the media are engaged in a legitimate activity when they stage-manage politics for the public. Communication through stage-management is unavoidable, since by far the great majority of the public in the media age can only come to grips with politics through the "languages" of the media. The languages of the media and especially of television, however, put a premium on the theatrical aspect of events, and more broadly on the elements most perceptible to the senses. The danger therein is that, in borderline cases, they will become entirely self-absorbed and self-referential, more preoccupied with the visual appeal of news-reporting than with the news itself. Viewers will see fine dramatic images devoid of information: circles of chattering, carping dignitaries, still photos of legislative chambers or meeting venues as a backdrop for the celebrities hurrying to, into, and out of press conferences and political engagements, follow-up personality stories in the wake of great events, communiqués from party conventions and much more.

Appropriateness concerns both the supply of political programming and the way the media rearranges and stages it. In either case appropriate material would have to meet two requirements. Political coverage should present themes that are relevant to the actual events, and should be sufficiently substantive as measured by the internal logic of the matters being covered. For media-users there should be a goal of at least minimum intelligibility guiding media language-use and production standards. As empirical studies have shown, there is no inherent structural barrier that would prevent media productions from following these guidelines for appropriate programming. Yet at present only a limited amount of media fare conforms to these guidelines, mainly for economic reasons.

If citizens' review boards were set up to exercise oversight over the media, there would be much more appropriate material. Civil society has its own ways of defining and developing media-worthy themes. Once mobilized, it too could have an indirect impact on the media on behalf of appropriateness guidelines, or for that matter even a direct impact if its members chose to launch campaigns directed explicitly at media decisions. But it is the public itself that could exert the greatest influence on both the media and politics, if it would indulge its taste for entertainment and good productions while never forgetting the difference between empty packaging and genuine content. Media literacy surely emerges on its own, but it would be far more appropriate for media democracy if we made it the core element in an educational canon in every sector of the educational system, just as reading and writing were long ago in the age of Gutenberg. This, together with a mobilized civil society consistently willing to challenge the narrow application of media codes across a wide spectrum of issues, could contribute to a more politically sophisticated communicative culture in the media. But it could also help to preserve political space for democratic parties, and to free politics itself from excessive dependence on the rules of the media stage.

Notes

Preface: Media, Culture, and Politics

1 Scannell/Schlesinger/Sparks (1992); Curran/Gurevitch (1996); Morley (1992); Corner (1997); Moores (2000).
2 Habermas (1996b); Dahlgren (1995); Graber (1990); Graber/McQuail/Norris (1998).
3 Corner (1997); Dahlgren/Sparks (1991); Scannell (1996); Curran/Seaton (1998).
4 Dahlgren/Sparks (1991), p. 17.
5 Dahlgren (1995).
6 Graber/McQuail/Norris (1998), pp. 71–144; Perloff (1998), pp. 185–264; Lang/Lang (1983); Lang/Lang (1984).
7 Curran/Smith/Wingate (1987); Dahlgren/Sparks (1992); Dahlgren (1995); Luhmann (1996).
8 Hall (1980); Graber (1998), pp. 145–204; Morley (1992); Morley (2000).
9 Staton (1994); Lance/Entman (2001); Schechter/Schatz (2001).
10 Robinson (1976); Holtz-Bacha (1990).
11 Patterson (1993); Norris (2000).
12 Viswanath/Finnegan (1996).
13 Hall (1980); Morley (1992); Bryant/Zillmann (1994).
14 Fiske (1987).
15 Hall (1980); Morley (1992).
16 Blumler/Katz (1974).
17 Corner (1999), p. 4
18 Morley (1980); Durham/Kellner (2001).
19 Postman (1985); Barber (1996), pp. 88–99.
20 Edelman (1976); Curran/Smith/Wingate (1987), p. 143.
21 Schwartzenberg (1980); Sarcinelli (1987); Meyer (1992).

22 Edelman (1976); Edelman (1988).
23 Dahlgren/Sparks (1991), p. 17.
24 Franklin (1992); Buchanan (1996); Jamieson (1996); Jarren/Schatz/ Weßler (1996); Dennis (1998); Lance/Entman (2001).
25 Schwartzenberg (1980); Grossman (1995).
26 Such analyses are in most cases restricted to the policy process and not extended to the dimension of politics as a whole.
27 Staton (1994).
28 Meyer/Ontrup/Schicha (2000); Rager/Rinsdorf/Bodin (2000); Meyer/ Schicha/Brosda (2001).
29 Asher (1995).
30 Fishkin (1991).
31 Graber (1990); Couldry (2000).
32 Keane (1984).
33 Melucci (1996); also Habermas (1996b).
34 Sarcinelli (1998).
35 Saxer (1998).
36 De Virieu (1990); Schechter/Schatz (2001).
37 De Virieu (1990); Schechter/Schatz (2001).
38 Schulz (1990); Jones (1996); Lance/Entman (2001).

Chapter 1   The Logic of Politics

1 Dahl (1998).
2 Dahlgren (1995), p. 4.
3 Ray (1973).
4 Schulz (1966); Sartori (1987).
5 De Tocqueville (1945).
6 Schumpeter (1942); Downs (1957).
7 Bachrach/Botwiniek (1992).
8 Barber (1984; 1996).
9 Panebianco (1988); Budge/Keman (1990).
10 Sarcinelli (1998), pp. 273–296.
11 Neidhardt (1994).
12 Meyer/Ontrup/Schicha (2000).
13 Parsons (1951).
14 Boorstin (1963); Jones (1995).
15 Edelman (1976); Sarcinelli (1987); Meyer (1992).
16 Klingemann/Hofferbert/Budge (1994); Panebianco (1988).
17 Leibholz (1958).
18 Michels (1968).

Chapter 2   The Logic of Mass Media

1 Corner (1999), pp. 41–3.
2 Luhmann (1996).
3 Lang/Lang (1968; 1984).
4 Dahlgren/Sparks (1992); Gripsrud (1999).
5 Lang/Lang (1984).
6 Galtung/Holomboe Ruge (1965); Graber (1985).
7 Galtung/Holomboe (1965); Schulz (1990); Fuller (1996).
8 Dahlgren/Sparks (1992), p. 3.
9 Graber (1994); Jones (1995); Meyer/Kampmann (1998); Meyer/Ontrup/ Schicha (2000).
10 Cf. for the following list: Meyer/Kampmann (1998); Meyer/Ontrup/ Schicha (2000).
11 Keane (1984).
12 Barber (1996), pp. 137–54.
13 For the following data: Hachmeister/Rager (1997).
14 McManus (1994).
15 Schulz (1990).

Chapter 3   The Process of Colonization

1 Franklin (1992); Staton (1994); Grossman (1995); Swanson/Mancini (1996); Dennis (1998); Lance/Entman (2001).
2 Schmidt (1987).
3 Plasser (1985).
4 Norris (2000).
5 Eliasoph (1998), pp. 255–8.
6 Morley (1992).
7 Dörner (2001).
8 Dahlgren/Sparks (1992).
9 Schechter/Schatz (2001).
10 Habermas (1986), chapter VI, 2.
11 Graber (1990); Grossman (1995); Graber/McQuail/Norris (1998).
12 Edelman (1988).
13 Swanson/Mancini (1996); Lance/Entman (2001).
14 Jones (1995); Tumber (2000); Whillock (2000).
15 Grossman (1995).
16 Ludes (1993).
17 Schwarzenberg (1980); Meyer/Ontrup/Schicha (2000).
18 Goffman (1959).

19 Smith (1980).
20 Edelman (1976; 1988; 2001).
21 Meyer/Kampmann (1998).
22 Fischer-Lichte (1994).
23 Boorstin (1963).
24 Jones (1995).
25 Burke (1992), pp. 236–42.
26 Edelman (1976); also: Kertzer (1988).

Chapter 4   The Effects of Colonization

1 Meyer/Schicha/Brosda (2001).
 2 Edelman (1988); Kepplinger (1996).
 3 Dahlgren/Sparks (1992), pp. 1–21.
 4 Dörner (2001).
 5 Kurbjuweit (2000).
 6 Kurbjuweit (2000), pp. 28–34.
 7 Kurbjuweit (2000).
 8 Kurbjuweit (2000), p. 34.
 9 Kurbjuweit (2000).
10 Dahlgren/Sparks (1992); Grewenig (1993); Meyer/Brosda/Schicha (2001).
11 De Tocqueville (1945), p. 106.
12 Sennett (1986).
13 Keane (1984).
14 Staton (1994); Blumler/Gurevitch (1995).
15 Meyrowitz (1985).
16 Jarren/Arlt (1997), p. 486.

Chapter 5   The Transformation of Representative Democracy

1 Cf. e.g. Bennett/Entman (2001).
 2 Patterson (1993); Niedermayer (1999).
 3 Meyer (1999).
 4 Dahlgren (1995), pp. 151–2.
 5 Curran/Smith/Wingate (1987), p. 143.
 6 Riddell (1998).
 7 Negrine (1994).

Chapter 6   Prospects for
Media Democracy

1 Dertouzos (1997); Bonchek (1997); Leggewie/Maar (1998).
2 Putnam (2000), pp. 166–80.
3 Scannell (1989), p. 161.
4 Corner (1999), p. 114.
5 De Virieu (1990).
6 Norris (2000). The affluence of empirical data in Norris's study notwith-standing, the author's key argument suffers from two weaknesses: first, the concept of practical political knowledge is too poor to cover appropriate understanding of what is going on in the political process. Second, "the virtuous circle" is just a new word to express the long-standing insight that only those who are highly motivated and well informed already and, in addition, make use of a broad variety of different media outlets will gain from what the media present as political information.
7 Schulz (1993); Patterson (1997); Kepplinger (1998); Putnam (2000), ch. 13.
8 Eliasoph (1998).
9 Grewenig (1993); Meyer/Ontrup/Schicha (2000); Dörner (2001).
10 Postman (1985).
11 Morley (1992); Dahlgren/Sparks (1992).
12 Habermas (1986).
13 Cohen (1988); Fishkin (1991).
14 Habermas (1996).
15 Dahlgren (1995).
16 Melucci (1996); Habermas (1996b), ch. 8.

Bibliography

Asher, H. 1995: *Polling and the Public. What Every Citizen Should Know*, 3rd edn. Washington, DC: CQ Press.

Bachrach, P. and Botwiniek, A. 1992: *Power and Empowerment: A Radical Theory of Participatory Democracy.* Philadelphia: Temple University Press.

Barber, B. R. 1984: *Strong Democracy. Participatory Politics for a New Age.* Berkeley: University of California Press.

Barber, B. R. 1996: *Jihad vs. McWorld.* New York: Ballantine Books.

Barber, B. R. 2000: *A Passion for Democracy.* Princeton, NJ: Princeton University Press.

Barber, J. D. 1980: *The Pulse of Politics. Electing Presidents in the Media Age.* New York: Norton.

Bennett, L. W. and Entman, R. M. (eds) 2001: *Mediated Politics. Communication in the Future of Democracy.* Cambridge: Cambridge University Press.

Blumler, J. G. and Katz, E. (eds) 1974: *The Uses of Mass Communications. Current Perspectives on Gratification Research*, 3rd edn. Beverly Hills: Sage.

Blumler, J. G. and Gurevitch, M. 1995: *The Crisis of Public Communication.* London: Routledge.

Blumler, J. G., Kavanagh, D. and Nossiter, T. J. 1996: Modern Communications versus Traditional Politics in Britain. In Swanson, D. and Mancini, P. (eds), *Politics, Media, and Modern Democracy. An International Study of Innovations in Electoral Campaigns and their Consequences.* Westport, CN: Praeger, pp. 49–72.

Bonchek, M. S. 1997: From Broadcast to Netcast. The Internet and the Flow of Political Information. Ph.D. thesis. Cambridge, MA: Harvard University.

Boorstin, D. 1963: *The Image or what Happened to the American Dream.* Harmondsworth, Middlesex: Penguin Books.

Bourdieu, P. 1996: *Sur la télévision, suivi de l'emprise du journalisme*, 17th edn. Paris: Liber.

Bryant, J. and Zillmann, D. (eds) 1994: *Media Effects. Advances in Theory and Research*. Hillsdale, NJ: Erlbaum.

Buchanan, B. 1996: *Renewing Presidential Politics: Campaigns, Media and the Public Interest*. Lanham, Md.: Rowman & Littlefield.

Budge, I. and Keman, H. 1990: *Parties and Democracy. Coalition Formation and Government Functioning in Twenty States*. Oxford: Oxford University Press.

Burke, P. 1992: *The Fabrication of Louis XIV*. New Haven/London: Yale University Press.

Burns, E. 1972: *Theatricality. A Study in Convention in the Theatre and Social Life*. London: Longman.

Clarke, P. (ed.) 1973: *New Models for Mass Communication Research*. Beverly Hills/London: Sage.

Cohen, J. L. 1988: Discourse Ethics and Civil Society. *Philosophy and Social Criticism*, 14(3–4): 315–37.

Corner, J. and Hawthorn, J. (eds) 1994: *Communication Studies. An Introductory Reader*, 4th edn. London: Arnold.

Corner, J. (ed.) 1997: *Popular Television in Britain. Studies in Cultural History*. London: BFI Publications.

Corner, J. 1999: *Critical Ideas in Television Studies*. Oxford: Clarendon Press.

Couldry, N. 2000: *The Place of Media Power. Pilgrims and Witnesses of the Media Age*. London: Routledge.

Curran, J., Smith, A. and Wingate, P. (eds) 1987: *Impacts and Influences. Essays on Media Power in the Twentieth Century*. London: Methuen.

Curran, J. and Gurevitch, M. (eds) 1996: *Mass Media and Society*, 2nd edn. London: Arnold.

Curran, J. and Seaton, J. 1998: *Power without Responsibility. The Press and Broadcasting in Britain*, 5th edn. London: Routledge.

Curtice, J. et al. 1999: *On Message. Communicating the Campaign*. London: Sage.

Dahl, R. 1998: *On Democracy*. New Haven/London: Yale University Press.

Dahlgren, P. and Sparks, C. 1991: *Communication and Citizenship. Journalism and the Public Sphere in the New Media Age*. London: Routledge.

Dahlgren, P. and Sparks, C. (eds) 1992: *Journalism and Popular Culture*. London: Sage.

Dahlgren, P. 1995: *Television and the Public Sphere. Citizenship, Democracy and the Media*. London: Sage.

De Tocqueville, A. 1945: *Democracy in America*. New York: Knopf.

De Virieu, F.-H. 1990: *La Mediacratie*. Paris: Flammarion.

Dertouzos, M. L. 1997: *What Will Be: How the New World of Information Will Change Our Lives*. San Francisco: Harper Edge.

Dörner, A. 2001: *Politainment*. Frankfurt/Main: Suhrkamp.

Downs, A. 1957: *An Economic Theorie of Democracy*. New York: Harper & Row.

Durham, G. M. and Kellner, D. M. 2001: *Media and Cultural Studies. Keyworks*. Malden, Mass.: Blackwell.

Edelman, M. 1976: *The Symbolic Uses of Politics*. Urbana: University of Illinois Press.

Edelman, M. 1988: *Constructing the Political Spectacle*. Chicago/London: University of Chicago Press.

Edelman, M. 2001: *The Politics of Misinformation*. Cambridge: Cambridge University Press.

Eliasoph, N. 1998: *Avoiding Politics. How Americans Produce Apathy in Everyday Life*. Cambridge: Cambridge University Press.

Fischer-Lichte, E. 1994: *Semiotik des Theaters. Eine Einführung*. Tübingen: Narr.

Fischer-Lichte, E. and Pflug, I. (eds) 2000: *Inszenierung von Authentizität*. Tübingen/Basel: Francke.

Fishkin, J. S. 1991: *Democracy and Deliberation. New Directions for Democratic Reform*. New Haven: Yale University Press.

Fiske, J. 1987: *Television Culture*. London/New York: Methuen.

Franklin, B. (ed.) 1992: *Televising Democracies*. London: Routledge.

Freedberg, D. 1989: *The Power of Images*. Chicago: University of Chicago Press.

Fuller, J. 1996: *News Values. Ideas for an Information Age*. Chicago/London: University of Chicago Press.

Galtung, J. and Holmboe Ruge, M. 1965: The Structure of Foreign News. The Presentation of the Congo, Cuba and Cyprus Crises in Four Norwegian Newspapers. *Journal of Peace Research*, 2: 64–91.

Garnham, N. 2000: *Emancipation, the Media, and Modernity. Arguments about the Media and Social Theories*. Oxford: Oxford University Press.

Goffman, E. 1959: *Presentation of Self in Everyday Life*. Garden City/New York: Doubleday.

Graber, D. A. 1985: Approaches to Content Analysis of Television News Programs. *Communications*, 11(2): 25–35.

Graber, D. A. (ed.) 1990: Media Power in Politics. *Congressional Quarterly*, 2. Washington, DC.

Graber, D. A. 1994: The Infotainment Quotient in Routine Television News: A Director's Perspective. *Discourse and Society*, 5(1994): 483–508.

Graber, D. A., McQuail, D. and Norris, P. (eds) 1998: *The Politics of News. The News of Politics*. Washington, DC: CQ Press.

Grewenig, A. (ed.) 1993: *Inszenierte Information. Politik und Strategische Kommunikation in den Medien*. Opladen: Westdeutscher Verlag.

Gripsrud, J. (ed.) 1999: *Television and Common Knowledge*. London: Routledge.

Grossman, L. K. 1995: *The Electronic Republic. Reshaping Democracy in the Information Age*. New York: Penguin Books.

Habermas, J. 1986: *The Theory of Communicative Action*. Boston: Beacon Press.

Habermas, J. 1996a: *Between Facts and Norms*. Cambridge, Mass.: MIT Press.

Habermas, J. 1996b: *Strukturwandel der Öffentlichkeit. Untersuchungen zu einer Kategorie der bürgerlichen Gesellschaft. Mit einem Vorwort zu Neuauflage*. Frankfurt/Main: Suhrkamp.

Hachmeister, L. and Rager G. (eds) 1997: *Wer beherrscht die Medien? Die 50 größten Medienkonzerne der Welt*. Munich: Beck.

Hall, S. 1980: 'Encoding/Decoding'. In Hall, S. (ed.), *Culture, Media, Language. Working Papers in Cultural Studies 1972–1979*. London: Hutchinson in association with the Centre for Contemporary Cultural Studies, University of Birmingham.

Holtz-Bacha, C. 1990: *Ablenkung oder Abkehr von der Politik?* Opladen: Westdeutscher Verlag.

Jamieson, K. (ed.) 1996: *The Media and the Politics*. Thousand Oaks: Sage.

Jarren, O. and Arlt, H.-J. 1997: Kommunikation – Macht – Politik. Konsequenzen der Modernisierung für die Öffentlichkeitsarbeit. *WSI Mitteilungen*, 7: 480–6.

Jarren, O., Schatz, H. and Weßler, H. (eds) 1996: *Medien und politischer Prozeß. Politische Öffentlichkeit und Massenmediale Politikvermittlung*. Opladen: Westdeutscher Verlag.

Jones, N. 1995: *Soundbites and Spin Doctors: How Politicians Manipulate the Media – and vice versa*. London: Cassell.

Keane, J. 1984: *Public Life and Late Capitalism*. Cambridge: Cambridge University Press.

Kepplinger, H. M. 1996: 'Inszenierte Wirklichkeiten'. *Medien und Erziehung*, 1: 12–23.

Kepplinger, H. M. 1997: *Die Demontage der Politik in der Mediengesellschaft*. Freiburg/Munich: Alber.

Kepplinger, H. M. 1998: *Die Demontage der Politik in der Informationsgesellschaft*. Freiburg (Breisgau)/Munich: Alber.

Kertzer, D. I. 1988: *Ritual, Politics & Power*. New Haven/London: Yale University Press.

Klingemann, H.-D., Hofferbert, R. J. and Budge, I. 1994: *Parties, Policies, and Democracy*. Boulder: Westview Press.

Kurbjuweit, D. 2000: *Der Spiegel. Reporter*, 6 Juni 2000: 28–33.

Lang, G. E. and Lang, K. 1983: *The Battles for Public Opinion. The President, the Press and the Polls during Watergate*. New York: Columbia University Press.

Lang, G. E. and Lang, K. 1984: *Politics and Television Re-viewed*. Beverly Hills, California: Sage.

Lang, K. and Lang, G. E. 1968: *Politics and Television*. Chicago: Quadrangle Books.

Leamer, L. 1984: *Make-believe: The Story of Nancy and Ronald Reagan*. New York: Dell.

Leggewie, C. and Maar, C. (eds) 1998: *Internet und Politik. Von der Zuschauer – zur Beteiligungsdemokratie*. Köln: Bollmann.

Leibholz, G. 1958: *Strukturprobleme der modernen Demokratie*. Karlsruhe: Müller.

Lenart, S. 1994: *Shaping Political Attitudes: The Impact of Interpersonal Communication and Mass Media*. Thousand Oaks, California: Sage.

Ludes, P. 1993: *Von der Nachricht zur News-Show*. Munich: Fink.

Luhmann, N. 1996: *Die Realität der Massenmedien*. Opladen: Westdeutscher Verlag.

Mancini, P. 1991: The public sphere and the use of news in a "coalition" system of government. In: Dahlgren, P. and Sparks, C. (eds), *Journalism and Popular Culture*. London: Sage.

Matalin, M. and Carville, J. 1995: *All's Fair. Love, War and Running for President*. New York: Random House.

McCarthy, J., Smith, J. and Zald, M. N. 1996: Accessing Public, Media, Electoral and Governmental Agendas. In: McAdam, D., McCarthy, J. D. and Zald, M. N. (eds), *Comparative perspectives on social movements: political opportunities, mobilizing structures, and cultural framings*. Cambridge/New York: Cambridge University Press.

McLuhan, M. 1994: *Understanding Media. The Extension of Man*. Cambridge/Mass.: The MIT Press.

McManus, J. 1994: *Market-Driven Journalism*. Newbury Park, CA: Sage.

Melucci, A. 1996: *Challenging Codes: Collective Action in the Information Age*. Cambridge: Cambridge University Press.

Meyer, T. 1992: Die *Inszenierung des Scheins. Voraussetzungen und Folgen symbolischer Politik*. Frankfurt/Main: Suhrkamp.

Meyer, T. and Kampmann, M. 1998: *Politik als Theater*. Berlin: Aufbau.

Meyer, T. 1999: From Godesberg to the Neue Mitte. The New Social Democracy in Germany. In Kelly, G. (ed.), *The New European Left*. London: Fabian Society.

Meyer, T., Ontrup, R. and Schicha, C. 2000: *Die Inszenierung des Politischen. Zur Theatralität von Mediendiskursen*. Wiesbaden: Westdeutscher Verlag.

Meyer, T., Schicha, C. and Brosda, C. 2001: *Diskursinszenierungen*. Wiesbaden: Westdeutscher Verlag.

Meyrowitz, J. 1985: *No Sense of Place. The Impact of Electronic Media on Social Behavior.* New York: Oxford University Press.

Michels, R. 1968: *Political Parties: A Sociological Study of the Oligarchical Tendencies of Modern Democracy.* New York: Free Press and Macmillan.

Moores, S. 2000: *Media and Everyday Life in Modern Society.* Edinburgh: Edinburgh University Press.

Morley, D. 1980: *The "Nationwide" Audience.* London: BFI Publications.

Morley, D. 1992: *Television, Audiences and Cultural Studies.* London: Routledge.

Morley, D. 2000: *Home Territories. Media, Mobility and Identity.* London: Routledge.

Morris, D. 1999a: *Behind the Oval Office. Getting Reelected against all Odds,* 2nd edn. Los Angeles: Renaissance Books.

Morris, D. 1999b: *The New Prince. Machiavelli Updated for the Twenty-first Century.* Los Angeles: Renaissance Books.

Müller, A. 1999: *Von der Parteiendemokratie zur Mediendemokratie. Beobachtungen zum Bundestagswahlkampf 1998 im Spiegel früherer Erfahrungen.* Opladen: Leske & Budrich.

Negrine, R. M. 1994: *Politics and the Mass Media in Britain,* 2nd edn. London: Routledge.

Negrine, R. M. 1998: *Parliament and the Media. A Study of Britain, Germany and the Media.* London: Pinter.

Neidhardt, F. (ed.) 1994: *Öffentlichkeit, öffentliche Meinung, soziale Bewegungen. Sonderheft Kölner Zeitschrift für Soziologie und Sozialpsychologie 34.* Opladen.

Niedermayer, O. 1999: Die Bundestagswahl 1998: Ausnahmewahl oder Ausdruck langfristiger Entwicklungen der Parteien und des Parteiensystems. In Niedermayer, O. (ed.), *Die Parteien nach der Bundestagswahl 1998.* Opladen: Westdeutscher Verlag.

Norris, P. et al. 1999: *On Message. Communicating the Campaign.* London: Sage.

Norris, P. 2000: *A Virtuous Circle: Political Communication in Post-Industrial Societies.* Cambridge: Cambridge University Press.

Panebianco, A. 1988: *Political Parties, Organization and Power.* Cambridge: Cambridge University Press.

Parsons, T. 1951: *The Social System,* 5th edn. New York: Free Press.

Patterson, T. E. 1993: *Out of Order.* New York: Knopf.

Patterson, T. E. 1997: The News Media. An Effective Political Actor? *Political Communication,* 14: 445–55.

Perloff, R. M. 1993: *The Dynamics of Persuasion.* Hillsdale, NJ: Erlbaum.

Perloff, R. M. 1998: *Political Communication. Politics, Press, and Public in America.* Mahwah, NJ/London: Erlbaum.

Plasser, F. 1985: Elektronische Politik und politische Technostruktur reifer Industriegesellschaften – Ein Orientierungsversuch. In Plasser, F., Ulram,

P. A. and Welan, M. (eds), *Demokratierituale. Zur politischen Kultur der Informationsgesellschaft.* Wien: Böhlau, 9–31.

Postman, N. 1985: *Amusing Ourselves to Death. Public Discourse in the Age of Show Business.* New York: Viking.

Putnam, R. 2000: *Bowling Alone. The Collapse and Revival of American Community.* New York: Simon & Schuster.

Rager, G., Rinsdorf, L. and Bodin, M. 2000: Theatralität und Argumentativität in der Mediengesellschaft (unpublished typescript). Dortmund: University of Dortmund, Institut für Journalismus.

Ray, M. L. 1973: Marketing Communication and the Hierarchy of Effects. In Clarke, P. (ed.), *New Models for Mass Communication Research.* Beverly Hills/London: Sage.

Riddell, P. 1998: Members and Millbank: the Media and Parliament. In Seaton, J. (ed.), *Politics and the Media,* 8–18.

Riddell, P. G. and Seaton, J. (eds) 1998: *Politics & The Media: Harlots and Prerogatives at the Turn of the Millennium.* Oxford: Blackwell.

Robinson, M. J. 1976: Public Affairs Television and the Growth of Political Malaise: The Case of the Selling of the Pentagon. *American Political Science Review,* 70: 409–32.

Ruddock, A. 2001: *Understanding Audiences. Theory and Method.* London/Thousand Oaks/New Delhi: Sage.

Sanders, D. et al. 1999: *On Message, Communicating the Campaign.* London: Sage.

Sarcinelli, U. 1987: *Symbolische Politik – Zur Bedeutung symbolischen Handelns in der Wahlkampfkommunikation der Bundesrepublik Deutschland.* Opladen: Westdeutscher Verlag.

Sarcinelli, U. 1998: Parteien und Politikvermittlung. In Sarcinelli, U. (ed.), *Politikvermittlung und Demokratie in der Mediengesellschaft.* Opladen/Wiesbaden: Westdeutscher Verlag, 273–96.

Sartori, G. 1987: *The Theory of Democracy Revisited.* Chatham/NJ: Chatham House.

Saxer, U. 1998: Mediengesellschaft. Verständnisse und Mißverständnisse. In Sarcinelli, U. (ed.), *Politikvermittlung und Demokratie in der Mediengesellschaft.* Opladen/Wiesbaden: Westdeutscher Verlag, 52–73.

Scammel, M. et al. 1999: *On Message, Communicating the Campaign.* London: Sage.

Scannell, P. 1989: Public Service Broadcasting and Modern Public Life. *Media, Culture and Society,* 11(2): 134–66.

Scannell, P., Schlesinger, P. and Sparks, C. (eds) 1992: *Culture and Power. A Media, Culture and Society Reader.* London: Sage.

Scannell, P. 1996: *Radio, Television and Modern Life. A Phenomenological Approach.* Oxford: Blackwell.

Schechter, D. and Schatz, R. (eds) 2001: *Mediaocracy "Hail to the thief": how the media "stole" the US presidential election 2000,*

MediaChannel.org, Media Tenor, WorldPaper. Bonn/Dover/Freiburg: Inno Vatio-Verl.

Schmidt, S. 1987: *Der Diskurs des Radikalen Konstruktivismus.* Frankfurt/ Main: Suhrkamp.

Schulz, E. B. 1966: *Democracy.* New York: Barron.

Schulz, W. 1990: *Die Konstruktion von Realität in den Nachrichtenmedien. Analyse der aktuellen Berichterstattung,* 2nd edn. Freiburg/Munich: Alber.

Schulz, W. 1993: Medienwirklichkeit und Medienwirkung. Aktuelle Entwicklungen der Massenkommunikation und ihre Folgen. In *Aus Politik und Zeitgeschichte.* Beilage zur Wochenzeitung das Parlament, B 40/93.

Schumpeter, J. A. 1942: *Capitalism, Socialism and Democracy.* London/New York: Harper & Brothers Publishers.

Schwartzenberg, R.-G. 1980: *L'Etat Spectacle.* Paris: Flammarion.

Seaton, J. (ed.) 1998: *Politics and the Media. Harlots and Prerogatives at the Turn of the Millennium.* Oxford: Blackwell.

Semetko, H. A. et al. 1999: *On Message, Communicating the Campaign.* London: Sage.

Sennett, R. 1986. *Die Tyrannei der Intimität. Verfall und Ende des Öffentlichen Lebens.* Frankfurt/Main: Fischer.

Shanahan, J. and Morgan, M. 1995: *Television and its Viewers. Cultivation Theory and Research.* Cambridge: Cambridge University Press.

Siune, K. (ed.) 1992: *Dynamics of Media Politics.* London: Sage.

Smith, H. 1980: *Reagan, The Man, The President.* New York: Macmillan.

Statham, P. 1996: Television News and the Public Sphere in Italy. Conflicts at the Media/Politics Interface. *European Journal of Communication,* 11: 511–56.

Staton, C. D. 1994: Democracy's Quantum Leap. *Demos Quarterly,* 3: 31–2.

Stephanopoulos, G. 1999: *All Too Human. A Political Education.* Boston/New York/London: Little, Brown.

Swanson, D. and Mancini, P. 1996: *Politics, Media, and Modern Democracy. An International Study of Innovations in Electoral Campaigning and their Consequences.* Westport, CN: Praeger.

Trent, J. S. and Friedenberg, R. V. 2000: *Political Campaign Communication: Principle and Practices,* 4th edn. Westport, CN: Praeger.

Tumber, H. (ed.) 2000: *Media Power, Professionals and Policies.* London/ New York: Routledge.

Verstraten, H. 1996: The Media and the Transformation of the Public Sphere. A Contribution for a Critical Political Economy of the Public Sphere. *European Journal of Communication,* 11: 347–70.

Viswanath, K. and Finnegan, J. 1996: The Knowledge Gap Hypothesis: Twenty-Five Years Later. In Burleson, B. and Kunkel, A. (eds), *Com-*

munication Yearbook 19. Thousand Oaks/London/New Delhi: Sage, 187–227.

Whillock, R. K. 2000: A Consultant's Angle: Comment On Politics and Politicians. *American Communication Journal*, 2(1).

Wieten, J., Murdock, G. and Dahlgren, P. 2000: *Television across Europe. A Comparative Introduction*. London: Sage.

Subject Index

Name Index